The Office of Eve

Surina Ann Jordan, PhD

authorHOUSE

AuthorHouse™
1663 Liberty Drive
Bloomington, IN 47403
www.authorhouse.com
Phone: 833-262-8899

Published by AuthorHouse 01/05/2023

ISBN: 978-1-6655-7826-4 (sc)
ISBN: 978-1-6655-7825-7 (hc)
ISBN: 978-1-6655-7827-1 (e)

Library of Congress Control Number: 2022923314

JGlobal Publishing
P.O. Box 65204
Baltimore, MD 21209
Edited by Naomi Books, LLC
Printed in the United States of America

Print information available on the last page.

Any people depicted in stock imagery provided by Getty Images are models,
and such images are being used for illustrative purposes only.
Certain stock imagery © Getty Images.

Unless otherwise indicated, scripture quotations are taken from the King James Version
(KJV) of the Bible, Broadman & Holman Publishers, Nashville, TN, 1996.

This book is printed on acid-free paper.

Because of the dynamic nature of the Internet, any web addresses or links contained in
this book may have changed since publication and may no longer be valid. The views
expressed in this work are solely those of the author and do not necessarily reflect the
views of the publisher, and the publisher hereby disclaims any responsibility for them.

My Gratitude Corner

Honoring my Adam, God the Father, God the Son (Jesus), God the Holy Spirit

<u>Helper Community</u>

Barbara Alexander

Paula Blake

Carol Brown

Lisa Crouse

Sheila Daniel

Naomi V. Dunsen-White

LuAnne E. Gilchrist

Yvette Harris

Margaret Hayes

Angela Hood

Mary Johnson

Pat Johnson

Ernestine Jones

Genesis J. Jordan

Shilo Nance

Gerri Pinkett

Fran Roach

Kelly Swanston

Prayer Circles

Prayer Partners

Men

Herbert Jordan III
Stephen Schwartz
Pastor P. M. Smith
Anthony Warren
Michael Williams

Cloud Family (Deceased)

Robert Thomas Coleman, Sr., and Lavenia Lovely Coleman
Herman Palmer and Edith Palmer
Barbara Pembamoto
Jacqueline Portlock

Contents

Foreword

In my bride's first book, *Got Cancer? Congratulations! Now You Can Start Living,* she took a cancer diagnosis (which most people associate with a death sentence) and made it a wake-up call to live life and live it more abundantly!

In her second book, *The Seven Disciplines of Wellness: The Spiritual Connection to Good Health,* she took wellness (which in too many minds looks like disease management) and made it a biblically based, common sense, lifestyle motivated by love and relationship!

In her third book, *Living Well: A Series of Short Articles for Holistic Living,* using a collection of natural health articles written when she was a columnist, Surina (in less than fifty pages), dispensed life-changing, easily digestible, nuggets of truth concerning topics ranging from natural beauty and weight loss to sleep, hygiene, healthy eating, and understanding environmental health.

Now in her latest book, The Office of Eve, she helps married and single women (Eves) thrive in a culture that is allergic to God. She helps answer the very important questions: "Why I am here?" and "What is my purpose?" Spoiler alert: all women (single or married) are Helpers.

The concept of a Helper, as developed in the book, is profound, empowering and liberating. It supplies a simple-to-grasp alternative to the world's, too often demeaning, devaluing, and objectifying depiction of women. It supplies a solution to the root cause of almost all marital problems: leadership. It also answers the question, "What's a single woman to do?"

Put simply, this is a book for married and single Eves and the men who would dare to love them and make them their brides! Thirty-two years ago, I was one of those men. Dr. Jordan told me, "If it came down to a choice between you and Jesus, you would finish a distant second." I could tell she meant it. With that statement, she established herself as an Eve and as my Helper. I had the good sense to marry her. For thirty-one years now, I wake up and choose to love my Eve, my Helper, more than I did the day before.

Herbert Jordan III

INTRODUCTION

- Who Should Read This Book
- Prayer Toolkit
- Glossary of Terms

Introduction

Welcome to the Office of Eve, a dimension of "who women *were* versus who they *have become*." This office operates as a fine-tuned, organized entity that works well by faith in the God who is. This office is a spiritual designation, by faith, that puts a woman of God right in the happenings of all things kingdom related. Married to Christ or married to an earthly Adam, Eve is a Helper, reporting to Holy Spirit, on assignment with purpose.

> **Main Point:**
>
> Eve is a Helper, reporting to Holy Spirit, on assignment with purpose.

Who Should Read This Book?

Females who:

- Want to know their place in God's plan for their lives
- Desire to uncover the deception implemented to derail the plan for their lives

Men who:

- Seek to know what is expected of them from the Word of God
- Want to get prepared for a real Eve
- Desire to understand their role with all the Helpers in their lives

Church Leaders who:

- Want to enhance their knowledge of scripture concerning Helpers
- Want to be prepared for effective ministry to Adams and Helpers, married and unmarried.

Anyone who:

- Wishes to grow from a deeper understanding of God's plan of creation for the world, using the office of Help.

Prayer Toolkit

At the back of this book, you will find the Prayer Toolkit, which offers simple prayers to assist you as you learn to better recognize the voice of Holy Spirit. It is my hope that you will be led to these prayers during your reading. Keep your heart open to receive, as the Lord's altar has been prepared for you, in Jesus' Name.

Office of Eve (OOE) — Glossary of Terms

Adam — Son of God, Jesus' younger brother, gifted in Christ by faith to bring love and power and good to the earth. All males are Adam, but not all Adams are leaders.

Assignment — a work or project a Helper is given or sometimes falls into. The goal is to solve a problem or bring life to a situation.

Engagement — a commitment, but not a covenant under God.

Eve — a Helper who is a reconnected believer in the Lord Jesus Christ, through salvation, who has asked for and received wisdom from God, which supernaturally increases the quality of her Help in all her assignments. She is a good and perfect gift from God the Father.

Helper — A female human, naturally created to help, which is their only purpose in life.

In Jesus' Name — Jesus is The Way to God. You would not want God to respond to you without Jesus, His Son. God's raw, unbuffered response would be so powerful, holy, and righteous that we could not survive it. Always in Jesus' Name. Amen.

Married, marriage, marry —

1. A covenant relationship under God between a Helper and an Adam.
2. A spiritual attachment to Jesus, in which He commits to care for and love a Helper.
3. A spiritual/physical attachment to an Adam, in which he commits to care for and love a Helper.

My Jesus — the husband (leader and protector) of all Helpers who are in Christ.

Wisdom — In Christ, it is the intelligence of God to see, make judgments, and use facts for the good. This form of wisdom is not used for God's purposes. The Apostle Paul refers to it as "worldly wisdom" in I Corinthians 1:19-31 and Colossians 2:8.

Your Jesus — a distinction of our Lord who has accepted your assignment to Him as His Helper.

CHAPTER 1

Entering the Office

My Journey to the Office of Eve

CHAPTER 1

Entering the Office

My Journey to the Office of Eve

First, I did not know what I did not know, which is what I believe is happening to generations of men and women. I am amazed at the patience and work of God the Father for each of us. His strategy to lovingly get me to this point in life is something to behold.

As a single woman, I was quite caught up in the life I thought was most promising and rewarding. I was a working professional (great corporate job), a college student, and had a few friends who could show me the "city life." I loved the clubs, dancing, sipping wines, and high-fashion dressing. I was one of the beautiful people. With God's favor, I was on a good career path. I honored my mom and dad by not exposing them to my less *godly* side. Looking back at it, I am sure Mom and Dad saw me and loved me through it.

Gently, I put my commitment to the Lord Jesus Christ on hold. I had opened so many doors to the enemy, and I am convinced that the grace of God and praying parents protected me. I did not even realize I needed protection. So, I went along, Jesus aside, picking up religion in all shapes and sizes. Over time, I became a Presbyterian, Baptist, Methodist, AME Methodist, and affiliated with several nondenominational churches. I even attended Holy Eucharist at the Catholic church, located around the corner from my downtown apartment in the city of Philadelphia.

All this experience was a great presentment of potential faith in Christ and lots of good, but each experience seemed to land me in the "no power zone" of the church. I prayed a little and read the Word a little, almost daily, and worshipped on Sunday, but was not lit with the power of God. I was unfaithful. There appeared to be many of us who were double minded in the faith, so I was in good company.

One day, Jesus broke through the guilt, shame, and blinded eyes of my life, and I completely embraced being *fully committed* and faithful to Christ.

Today, I have been happily married to my husband for over thirty years. Prior to this assignment, I sought the Lord, not really understanding Holy Spirit's *help* in my life. When I committed my life to Christ, I married *Him* first, and He began to direct my path. I remember being led to pray specific prayers. For example, *Lord, I do not want anything to separate me from You again. How do I pick this guy?* (See Prayer Toolkit.) He showed me celibacy as a common practice, based on a believer's spiritual connectedness to Christ. My faithfulness to Christ was an opportunity to understand faithfulness to my future *Adam*.

My wonderful Adam and I were friends and coworkers for over ten years prior to marriage. When we started dating (around year eleven), we decided to go to dinner one night. While we were chatting, he asked me the perfect question! No, it was not, "Will you marry me?" Rather, it was, "So, what do I need to do to get Christ?" He gave his life to Christ right there during our dinner date! It was a life-changing event for him. He was a good man who did not have Jesus, and at that moment, he had received Jesus and became one of the sons of God.

I have had an interesting view of Eve (the Helper) in my life. My grandmother was a woman of God, who walked well in her Eve anointing. She and her husband (Grandad) adopted my mom. I never witnessed her being quick to speak or becoming angry. Nor had I ever heard her criticize my grandad or dishonor him. She passed away, after Grandad did, when I was thirty-three years old and single.

My mother married her Sunday school teacher, my dad. It was not an immediate connection, but I will not impose all the details on you. She was a wonderful mother and wife, and my parents had eight children. However, looking back, my mom did not always walk in her Eve office. A real helper she was, but the wisdom that comes with the Office of Eve was not there.

Mom was an only child and lacked nothing, including knowing how to get her way. Seeing how she related to her husband (my dad) was how I learned that your husband could be overridden and disrespected when you needed to have something done your way. But in my mom's defense, no one taught her that her power in life was directly related to her prayer life, which was where she needed to take all of Dad's shortcomings and concerns. Dad had some big ministry goals and entrepreneurial aspirations that needed an Eve Helper in position. My mom did not see this clearly. A Helper without the leadership and understanding of Holy Spirit can hinder Adam's vision.

It was not until I could not do things for *my* children that I realized it was *not* my role to do some things I would do. There are some things fathers need to do, like attending school events, tucking the children in at bedtime, having final words with them about their day, and praying over them.

It has been several years since I ruptured a blood vessel in my brain. (See "My Testimony: The Story of the Great Bleed" in the rear of this book). God has been merciful to me. Now I see that my healing has much to do with my will to live and serve in the Office of Eve for my Adam and our household, to the glory of God the Father.

This is one of many redeeming scriptures for me: "And we know that all things work together for good to them that <u>love God</u>, to them who are the <u>called</u> according to <u>his purpose</u>." (Romans 8:28). I love God and have been called to be a Helper. He used His Word and the good all around me and within me to work through my ignorance of the deeper meaning of the *call*. My call is to the Office of Eve.

I realized I had stunted my Adam's growth with my out-of-control disobedience to God. A lot of his struggle over the years was there because of my not being in place to help him and because of my ignorance and misalignment with the Word of God. So now, I am in line to be that wise woman (Proverbs 31), who is Eve.

Even now, there are some things within my old nature that, thankfully, the Father is rooting out of me, according to scripture in Matthew 15:13. Now I can fuss and vent to Holy Spirit, and I can sit and meditate on things, as Holy Spirit makes them plain to me. For example, I had put my mind and effort into preparing a great next-step project for my Adam's household. In my mind, all I needed was his signature and we would be set to move forward. He would not do it! His point was that he could not do it until I was visibly healed. He saw things in my rehabilitation that he could do better and put in place to advance my healing and well-being. He did not feel that God was going to be pleased if he did not put my well-being first. He said my wholeness (just like Christ loving on the church), is more important than anything or any *stuff.* The Helper in me does not agree with this, for in my mind, I will be healed and made whole eventually, as I help. However, as I sat complaining about this situation to Holy Spirit, the Father reminded me that in the oneness of our relationship, He honors Adam and will bless Adam's way as he leads. This was a major enlightenment for me. Adam's way is rarely my way. However, I am a Helper, *not* his leader.

This was the first time I did not jump into my "I can do this" nature, using my skills, knowledge, and whatever else to make it all happen perfectly! As my soul prospers, I see that my Adam puts me first, even when I do not see the need. That is scripture. I must be okay that the train will slow down as he handles and processes things. I am *on* the train, not *driving* the train. I am here to help, not to lead. This was so difficult for me until I was able to see through God's Word, my placement in God's order of things. God's order has not changed.

I am so thankful and amazed at the life God has afforded me while I was unaware of my role, image, and spiritual designation in Him.

It should be noted that if you are going to the scriptures to look for gender equality, based on our culture, you will be surprised to discover that men and women are not the same. We are not equal, and we never will be. Other places in our world see it differently. However, in scripture, it is not about equality, superiority, or rank.

In the Kingdom of God, each of us has a divine assignment. We were not created to do the same things or be equal. But we are all created to be of great worth and value to the Lord God. God still sees us this way. Our value is diminished as we attempt to become like someone else and fight for our right to be what we have chosen for ourselves (with help from the deceiver).

Life using God's plan is amazingly fulfilling and complete.

Prayer Agreement

Father, in Jesus' Name, thank You for this revelation word, knowledge, and understanding that point me to purposeful living and reveals where I am and who I am in Christ. Let this word become real to me. Spring up a well in me and use me to bring glory to You. Amen.

Main Point:

My faithfulness to Christ was an opportunity to understand faithfulness to my future Adam.

CHAPTER 2

Human Helper

Human Helper

A Helper is the most powerful female in the universe. Handmade and heavily influenced by God, Holy Spirit, she is not a copy of Adam. God used Adam's DNA to establish the lineage, spiritual position, and value for this second human. (Genesis 2:22). As part of her body design, she was given a womb with built-in feeding and the essential elements of human capacity to build a household, give birth to Adam's seed, and prepare them to live in the world. In the natural, she is also a businesswoman, mom, executor of dreams, wife, and leader. She has a very fruitful sphere of relationships, including family, friends, prayer partners, and church fellowship for growing faith and maintaining her overall health.

Married couples must be under God and renewed by Christ. They have become one. If ever there are two heads, it is a big open door for the enemy of God to enter. So, God chose the man, His son, to love and lead within the presence of God. Adam's love for Eve mirrors Christ's love for the Church. It does not mean destructive freedoms or abuse for anyone. Marriage is about all-around servanthood.

Adam is a *son of God* king (small *k*). Adam, in the spirit realm, is Christ's younger brother. God sees him as His son. (Romans 8:14, John 1:34). Adam must know and love his Father (God) before he can receive and love a Helper.

Adam seeks wisdom and suggestions regarding his work from his Helper. He considers her words, needs, and desires. He does not treat her as if she does not have a voice or as if she were a child. Adam clearly understands his gift in Eve, and like Christ with the Church, he handles her as a precious gift.

Helper value is demonstrated in a story in scripture. (I Samuel 30:1-19). David and his men returned home to find that the Amalekites had invaded the south, destroyed Ziklag and burned it with fire. They had also captured, alive, the wives of David and his men. He and his men were so sorrowful; they wept until they could not weep anymore. These men were sick with grief and angry with David. Their Helpers, households and legacies had been taken away. David went to God for assistance in regaining their Helpers. God allowed David to recover them all.

In today's culture, some women will not agree with this view of women. However, a woman of God who does not agree with this word should go directly to the Word of God for understanding, not to validate her own way, but for revelation. A Helper who is married has a primary assignment to her husband. Her role in that relationship is to understand and intercede in prayer for "her Adam." The term "her Adam" or "my Adam" denotes that her assignment from God to Adam is a lifelong relationship, permitting them to be productive (fruitful) together in every good way. They have vision, faith, and the collective abilities to complete the work. The bottom line is every female who is and ever will be — is a Helper. (Genesis 2:18).

Many Helpers are married to Christ instead of being married to an Adam. Helpers have many assignments; being married to an Adam is only one of them. As individuals, this population of human Helpers has a tremendous capacity to do whatever they are assigned to do. Even a married Helper, assigned to an Adam and his household, eventually develops the capacity to take on more assignments. It is in her nature to go and do. Married Helpers are being renewed to stand strong and ready to help carry the presence of Christ all over the world, including to family, community, state, country, and beyond.

Helpers married to Jesus can respond more to the "go ye" as Jesus instructed: "Go ye therefore, and teach all nations, baptizing them in the name of the Father, and of the Son, and of the Holy Ghost:" (Matthew 28:19). She does not have an assignment to an Adam and can be solely focused on her calling to help the cause of Christ.

Main Point:

Every female who is and ever will be — is a Helper.

CHAPTER 3

Helper for God

- Masterful Deception Eve
- Helper Distinction
- The Helper Community
- Helper Beauty
- Who is Eve?
- The Nature of Eve
- Attributes of the Office of Eve
- Helper, Daughter of God
- Growing Your Soul to Good Health
- Wise Woman
- Wise Woman Disposition
- Helper Benefit Package
- Short Stories of Helpers and Eves
- Helpers Who are Leaders
- Helpers from All Ethnic Origins
- Widows
- Helper, Detached From God
- Life With God Must be Restored

Helper for God

Masterful Deception of Eve

T he struggle is over. The veil of deception has been lifted.

There is a common perception that the only human Helper (Eve) was an airhead. She was not. She was deceived by God's enemy, the devil, or Satan. Satan never saw her as stupid. It was deep, dark deception he used. Even today, this type of manipulation and coaching is not easily detected without help from Christ. Christ's death and resurrection eliminated the deceiver's ability to steal, kill, and destroy those who believe.

Ephesians 2:2 refers to Satan as the "prince of the power of the air," which indicates a vast stolen dominion being utilized to plant any negative source of information. This dominion uses imagery, audio, and print, supported by an ungodly language, which shapes, values, and builds memories that do not agree with God. This dominion has thick layers of darkness, with fruitful wickedness in high places. (Ephesians 6).

Industry, economies, and multimedia are all plugged in to infiltrate fear and confusion. It uses facts, studies, and money to shape value systems and the protocol for wonderfully appealing, ungodly behaviors. This process is so smooth that it must be right.

For those "on the fence" regarding righteousness, they do not stand a chance at seeing the deception that leads to a life without God. Here are some other points of deception that get planted into our value system:

Point of Deception	Deceiver's End Game (Goal)
You are not complete; God made a mistake with you.	Constantly comparing oneself with others. Breeds self-hate and gender confusion.
There is always something that goes wrong.	Looking for, expecting, and being fearful of a negative. "What next?" becomes the norm.
Adam or not, I will work to please whomever I choose.	Helpers not properly assigned can help themselves to death via cancer, obesity, etc.
Women are okay on their own.	Women can end up in vulnerable situations. (Depending upon unjust laws for protection.)
I must be beautiful at all costs.	The uniqueness of every creature is overridden, and beauty is redefined toward pornography.
Children know as much as parents.	Lead parents to let their children run their own lives.
All men are dogs, but I need one to make me whole.	Men are not important. You need a utility, not an Adam.
It is okay to show off my body parts, even the private ones.	You must do this to be attractive and stand out. There is too much competition.
I can raise some children and terminate others.	Loving and caring for pets is easier. The unborn innocent suffer.
Things are more important than people.	Real *important* stuff comes first.

In my younger adult days, aborting a baby was hardly even connected to taking a life or killing a person. It was an outpatient medical procedure called a D and C (Dilation and Curettage), which is a multi-use/multi-purpose scraping of the uterus, the most sacred place for a child. It was fully covered by my medical insurance — smooth deception. I never saw the strategy to derail the course of a Helper and discard a life. Helpers do not see that having unmarried sexual relations is violating a key law of being fruitful under God. I did this twice! The job of discarding this child (seed) appears to be the responsibility of the Helper (not the man) to do the killing. A similar deception is told in the scriptures through the story of the adulterous woman. (John 8:1-11). She was not pregnant, but was caught in the "very act" and was about to be stoned. No man was taken or held responsible, only the Helper was accused. Unjust laws in the land make it easy to kill, destroy the innocent, and help manage wrongdoings.

Adultery was also a very smooth deception for me. I was of the mind that men who approached me were available like I was, and I did not even realize they were married until I was already involved. It was very smooth because I had a full-time job and went to college full time. I was so busy that I did not even notice how little time that person had for me. I never even thought of the household I was being spiritually inserted into and how much evil was being poured into innocent lives as a result.

So, like the Apostle Paul, I (the *redeemed* me) never did these things. That was the other Surina. If God can fix me, He can fix anybody. No fear, shame, guilt, or condemnation. Jesus carried it all in His body on a tree for me and you. I am forgiven. (I Peter 2:24, Romans 6:11).

I am a daughter of the living God. I am dressed in righteousness and stand upright before the Father because of The Way made by Jesus, who is Christ, my Lord, Savior, and elder brother. I am heir to the throne. I am Eve. (Romans 8:14).

> **Main Point:**
>
> The veil of deception has been lifted.

Helper Distinction

Now, in Christ, I have total and complete freedom. I am an anointed Helper, aligned with the Holy Spirit of God. A daughter of the Father and Helper with God, the Holy Spirit.

In the creation story, man was made in the image of God. God saw that even He has a Helper, a part of the Holy Trinity, God, Holy Spirit. When He considered the work He had given to Adam, God said, "… It is not good that the man should be alone; I will make him an help meet for him." (Genesis 2:18). I believe the Holy Spirit of God, the Helper, was actively involved in the creation of this — the first and only human Helper. Her spiritual designation is connected to God, the Helper. *This is the foundation for the Office of Eve, a* Helper who is reconnected to The Holy Helper through Christ. This is different from Adam's designation. Adam is a son of God, like Jesus, his older brother.

When Satan saw this unbelievable Helper with all the divine wonder in human form, he decided he had to have her.

All female humans are Helpers, ever ready to help. **Eve** is the wise Helper who is Holy Spirit infused and assigned to help. She uses the Word of God and asks for the wisdom of God to come into her heart. An Eve who has the spirit of wisdom is a powerful one, helping and resting in God. If the world had more Eves, it would be a good and different place.

Helpers were not designed to stand alone. They attach to people and organizations to help. The first divine assignment for a Helper is to connect to Jesus Christ. God made sure to offer this Christ connection to Helpers for salvation, leadership, and protection. Jesus not only died for *her* sins, but He also agreed to cover *every* Helper by marrying her. When I refer to Jesus *marrying* a woman, I mean that once she accepts Christ as her Lord and Savior; she is in a covenant relationship with Him. As a Helper, this relationship is the training ground, the preparation, for her covenant with an earthly Adam. Therefore, if a Helper never has an earthly Adam, she is always covered by Christ, and by faith, must understand the Word of God concerning this. (I Corinthians 7:34).

If you have not accepted Christ into your heart, you will need to do this first. Accept Jesus Christ as your Lord and Savior, and then this discussion will make more sense to you. (See Extra Help for Helpers (A) Connect to Christ.) You will be made whole: body, mind, and spirit.

So, wherever you are in life, let this knowledge open your eyes of understanding. Let this revive your spirit. Receive the wisdom and confidence in your place within the Kingdom of God. Contrary to what the enemy would have you think, you are not an afterthought. You are not a second fiddle. You were there *in the beginning* also (the spiritual designation of Eve was there). You were given the great mandate, which is, "Be fruitful [productive] and increase in number; fill the earth and subdue it. Rule over the fish in the sea and the birds in the sky and over every living creature that moves on the ground." (Genesis 1:28 New International Version [NIV]).

Helpers need protection and wisdom. Helpers are best when they marry Christ. Helpers are also directly connected to the Chief Helper, God, Holy Spirit. He knows every ounce of her greatness and is postured to bring it out and present that part of her at the appropriate time. She has unlimited potential and purpose that no one can take away.

Every baby girl is born a Helper by the Father's design. The Father has made plans for all Helpers in the world to bring forth His kingdom on earth as it is in heaven. Each Helper has a special gift and special assignments. Is there anyone else in the world who can birth kings, leaders, and more Helpers? Eve does not have to bear children; however, she is the only human who is built and gifted to do so.

It is important that you embrace your purpose as God planned for you. (Jeremiah 29:11). See yourself as a spirit first. The physical wrap on you is not as important as the Helper within. The spirit and soul of you is the breath of life given by God, your Heavenly Father, so you reflect Him no matter who or where you are. You are designed by God for a particular purpose. That purpose is filled with love, joy, peace, confidence, and faith. It is a sad thing to see a Helper who does not understand this.

We meet our purpose first in the spirit realm. This is where God is. Remember the scripture that tells us, *they that come to the Father must come to Him in spirit and in truth.* (John 4:24). When you invite Christ into your heart and get baptized, your spirit is forever filled with love, healing, peace, and the power of the Holy Spirit of God. In this way, your understanding of what is important in life changes. You want good! You do good! You are good! And you are an Eve!

You begin to feel special. Your faith will allow you to feel the love. It may also feel strange in that you have never experienced this before. You no longer seek to be accepted by the *in* crowd. The promised rest and peace are invaluable.

Main Points:

- This is the foundation for the Office of Eve, a Helper who is reconnected to The Holy Helper through Christ.
- Your faith will allow you to feel the love.

The Helper Community

The Helper community is a division within the Kingdom of God that has an earthly physical realm. It consists of several billion human Helpers, connected to God, Holy Spirit, through Christ.

This human Helper is amazingly appealing to Satan. He used her to get to Adam, knowing that he could not get to Adam directly. Satan sought to harness her power and use her Helper nature to destroy. All other nonhuman Helpers are good spirits and good angels. Human Helpers are only women. All women are born Helpers, and many have specific marital and motherhood assignments laid out for them. However, marriage and motherhood are not the only assignments of Helpers. In every realm of society, you will find Helpers. God planned it this way.

As you study the Word of God, you will see that Helpers have been very effective in spreading the good news of Christ. For example, in scripture, the Helpers who gathered at Jesus' tomb, upon learning that He had risen, were instructed by the angel of the Lord, "But, go your way, tell…" (Mark 16:1-7). Note, he does not tell them to go on a missionary journey like the Apostles Paul or Peter or to drop every assignment they currently had. They are told to go in the direction that is their normal way and tell. Helpers *do* carry the gospel.

All over the world, Helpers who operate under the banner of Christ are actively serving God. Helpers get support from other Helpers who are led to connect for specific assignments, resources, information, and fellowship.

The seasoned Helpers are Eves, full of the wisdom and knowledge and the Love of God. These Eves help other Helpers. Women's ministries are good examples of Helper communities full of Eves, fortifying the community for their good and God's glory. These ministries must remain watchful and prayerful as Jesus warned, so they can stand ready, not be deceived, or distracted by the devil. (Mark 13:33).

Main Point:

The seasoned Eves help other Helpers.

Helper Beauty

I am a confident, wise woman. **My self-confidence** is a download of faith in God for His glory. That faith brings an outward appearance of hope, joy, and dignity to my face.

A good part about knowing my position is that I no longer must try to be beautiful. Beauty is already a part of me. I will naturally appeal and appear most attractive to the Adam who has my spiritual designation. I am a designer original. No one can ever be me!

My body is the temple of the Holy Spirit of God in Christ. Behold, all things are new, not different but new — not almost, but new. When your spirit and soul connect to Christ, then the body will come along as you grow in your relationship with Christ. What is the image of a temple of God, the human Helper?

The Human Helper:

1. Is guaranteed good health as her soul prospers. (III John 1:2).
2. Is not fashion-obsessed, but rather fashion-oriented, based on her assignment. Holy Spirit helps her with her package (outward presentation). She will gravitate to what compliments her.
3. Does not require big bucks. She needs only a few things that have value.
4. Is clean and neat. A well-groomed body temple represents God well. Any mirror work she does is with Holy Spirit's help and protection. This is important, so she does not entertain critical self-assessments or comparisons to the world's so-called *beautiful* people.
5. Looks as sacred and orderly as a temple. (I Corinthians 14:40).
6. Requires morning stretching and breathing. Daily dedication to God is essential.
7. Exhibits modest dressing. Based on her lifestyle, what does she need for every potential occasion? (I Timothy 2:9).
    a. Identify colors – She uses colors that enhance her skin tone. Some colors bring energy, others bring calm.
    b. Identify essentials she naturally gravitates to. For example:
       - The shapes and sizes that work best.
       - Items that fit into her day-to-day.
       - Simple and low maintenance.
8. Requires an organized process of body temple maintenance that must be set up by a Helper. She cannot require high maintenance for anything.

A Helper does not need to reveal her physical body, except to her Adam (husband). Discretion is key and very powerful. Men want to see, but they do not want to share their view. Any inappropriate use of revealed skin and tight clothing are like raw honey; it attracts all types of flies. The Kingdom of God has no need for the terms *sexy* or *arrogant*. Helpers are attractive and built with long-lasting dignity.

But know this: Helpers are very good at packaging. She must see herself as that unique package God has poured into her physical image. So, how she presents herself is a part of that unique package. This packaging is a good practice to show forth the glory of God, and how you, as a Helper, can manage the gifts of God and your upcoming assignments.

The goal in life concerning your appearance is to carry the expression of God exactly as He made you. You can bring up the beauty and fragrant your body temple; however, there is no need to recreate, dislike, or use ungodly enhancements. A Helper must be in spiritual and physical shape. Her countenance will be evident. In jeans and a tee shirt, her dignity and glow are impressive.

Finally, the best beauty secret I have to offer a Helper is to remain in the presence of The Holy (with God) as much as possible. I reflect His glow, His Joy, His Peace, and His strength, which corrects my posture. As I am with Him, my body temple is held whole.

Main Points:

- I reflect God's glow, His Joy, His Peace, and His strength, which corrects my posture.
- As I am with Him, my body temple is held whole.

Who is Eve?

Eve is the first and only human ever created to help. (Genesis 2:20). Eve is a multidimensional designation (spirit, mind, and body), created to bring balance and provide completion for all good works upon the earth. To glorify God with her life, her salvation in Christ establishes her office.

Her office is connected to the Spirit of Wisdom, which is the intelligence of God. In her position, she can provide the appropriate solution in every situation. She is Eve the Helper, full of wisdom and dignity.

When a Helper accepts Christ, she becomes Eve, which infuses these assignments with the power of the Holy Spirit of God. There are many assignments set up for Helpers. Some are listed below:

- Wise Women
- Wife
- Mother
- Single Married to Christ
- Single Mother Married to Christ
- Divorcée
- Widow
- Aunt
- Girl
- Cousin
- Sister
- Daughter
- Teacher
- Boss/Leader
- Caregiver

Main Point:

A female is the only human Helper. She becomes Eve when she accepts Jesus Christ as Lord and Savior. She also receives Jesus as her cover/protector (or her husband if she is unmarried).

The Nature of Eve

In Genesis 2:19, God and Adam were involved in some intense work relating to creation, earth maintenance, and empowerment. God made every living creature, and Adam named them. God noticed that Adam had much responsibility, but no help. Also, Adam needed someone to carry his seed in order to multiply (bear his children). He also needed wisdom and intelligence wrapped around each part of his massive responsibility. God poured Himself into a second being — this was Eve, the Helper.

He put Adam down and performed surgery to remove Adam's rib. Using that rib, God wrapped it in flesh. God then took the attributes of a special being like Adam, but sculpted it with tremendous femininity, stamina, and an angelic-like presence. He put His intelligence into every realm of her, making her a beautiful, soft, curvaceous structure. She was perfectly erect, with a crown of hair and brilliance. He then loaded her with everything Adam and the world would ever need to help keep his sphere and this world alive and able to thrive. God engrained in her the nature of a Helper, which is connected to God the Helper (Holy Spirit). Like her angelic partners, she looks to follow orders and responds to her leader (Adam or Christ). The Holy Spirit of God is available to do what is needed to protect and care for God's image, Adam and Eve, as they walk in the Truth, and The Life, moving in The Way, who is The Christ.

Eve is the Helper assigned to Adam and guided by the Holy Spirit of God. (John 14:26). Adam should expect constant wisdom and insight and solutions from her regarding his work and other issues. Holy Spirit carefully crafts questions, affirmations, and talking points (or cues) for Adam's needs. Adam should present his issues and challenges to God and to Eve (confidentially). It is the God in her doing the work, fulfilling her assignment for Him by faith, in the order of Melchizedek. (John 14:10).

God expects to hear from her on Adam's behalf. She completes him (spiritually, physically, and mentally) and helps to make him whole. Adam's thoughts and ideas have been connected to her relationship with God, through prayer and the oneness given to them in God's Word in Genesis 2:24. By faith, she brings to God all the needs (known petitions) and SOS (emergency petitions) being made for her Adam. She can be slow to speak, which creates enough silence for her to get the response and information from Holy Spirit for that situation. Based on scripture, she does not even have to teach or correct. She simply prays truthfully out of her emotions and lets Adam's head (God the Father) handle him. (I Timothy 2:12). Because of her connection to Holy Spirit, she can gently sustain the peace they enjoy. Their time together, at the park or in bed, is before the throne of God with His blessing. What joy!

"Adam was made first, then Eve; woman was deceived first—our pioneer in sin!—with Adam right on her heels. On the other hand, her childbearing brought about salvation..." (I Timothy 2:13-15 The Message [MSG]). She brought forth the new Adam – Christ, our Savior.

Historically, in Christendom, Adam the husband and Eve the wife, were the basic area of concentration which placed the unmarried population of individual humans on the sidelines. The deceiver is right there to infuse the feeling of being *rejects* or *damaged* goods or worse. Little seems to fit, and our culture appears to leverage this void in

Christianity to enforce a state of confusion and failures they attribute to God.

From motherhood to ministry, industry, and leadership, Helpers have always had powerful assignments. Satan, the enemy of God, has always sought to deceive and destroy this population of humans by keeping them away from the Father and not allowing them to have the proper image of themselves, which may hinder their ability to accomplish their assignments.

Main Point:

God engrained in her the nature of a Helper, which is connected to God the Helper (Holy Spirit).

Attributes of the Office of Eve

An important point of distinction is "born a Helper, always a Helper." Helpers can help anybody in any situation. Helpers do not change their minds about being Helpers; it has been innately ingrained into them. The supernatural chromosomal activity en route to the resting place in the womb, and the overall consideration for each human life determines whether the baby is a god-Helper (a girl) or a god (a boy). According to Psalm 139:14, there are no mistakes. So, this biological occurrence creates humans who must be spiritually connected to God through Jesus Christ to live eternally. Instead, they can live in a physical nature based on the reality of Satan, God's enemy, who has shaped the culture away from its proper spiritual alignment and rules of deception in the natural realm of life.

A Helper is the spiritual/physical designation of every female on earth. However, every Helper is not an Eve. Many Helpers are strangers to God. They function outside of their office. They can naturally do some good and much bad. They can self-implode by taking charge or overhelping. Helpers lack wisdom and they are vulnerable to the deceitful practices and suggestions from the devil. They can speak and plant so much death until their ways eventually put *them* to death. The most common diseases (obesity, cancer, hypertension, and diabetes) can be linked to Helpers crossing the emotional/spiritual guardrails that were established through Christ to keep them safe.

As we accept Christ into our hearts and request His Kingdom in our lives, all things become new. As you grow in this, you will see newness all throughout your life.

Main Point:

A Helper is the spiritual/physical designation of every female on earth.

Helper, Daughter of God

A Helper who is spiritually aligned with Christ has a stronger position in God's Kingdom and the world. She has a hedge of protection around her, keeping her safe in the physical realm and in the spiritual realm as well. This is so important for a Helper. Therefore, we see the level of pain, destruction, and deceit in the Helper population, because they are a threat to the enemy of God. I imagine that Satan was blown away when he saw what God poured into this human at creation.

If she connects with someone with bad intentions, she is most vulnerable. Her Helper nature can be misused, hurt, or damaged.

By nature, a Helper helps. Innately intelligent, she can do anything. A Helper assigned to a work must see the big picture of any assignment. She sees it all, which allows her to help at any point in the work. Not seeing her gift, she could unknowingly use it to take over, criticize, or step out of place, like Miriam, in scripture. She was an Eve, but lacked wisdom. She spoke out negatively about her brother, Moses. She was stricken with leprosy (a curse) and removed from the camp. (Numbers 12:1-15).

Yet the powerful part of this Helper office (in Christ) is that *she knows how to restrain herself, with all that knowledge, and only uses what is needed.* She uses critical points of restraint when she is capable of doing so much more.

Therefore, in the Office of Eve, a Helper is operating within the will of God. Scripture indicates that before you had lived one day, God considered you. (Psalm 139). So, before the biological event, as mentioned before, was completed, you became a package containing all you needed to finish your purpose and assignments. Do not be concerned if life looks so different, rough, or tough. God never changes His mind about His Helpers. His Word assures us of this: "For I know the thoughts that I think toward you, saith the LORD, thoughts of peace, and not of evil, to give you an expected end." (Jeremiah 29:11).

A Helper saved through Jesus Christ, reporting to Holy Spirit for assignment, does not have to be in a confused state. Her essential arsenal of power must include the Word of God. She is powerful and protected and living within the Kingdom of God. She has a hedge of protection against the kingdom of darkness and evil. She is no longer vulnerable to satanic attacks and agendas that keep her from glorifying God. She can ask for and receive Holy Spirit power, leadership, and wisdom.

Main Point:

The Office of Eve, therefore, is that of a Helper operating within the wisdom and will of God.

Growing Your Soul to Good Health

"Beloved, I wish above all things that thou mayest prosper and
be in health, even as thy soul prospereth." —III John 1:2

Along the journey to report for assignment, we must develop our soul, which is the inner person Christ redeemed. Holistically, our health is tied to the prospering of our soul. It is common sense and leads us to the path of being wise women. A wise woman has the energy (health and strength) of a prospering soul. This provides an accelerated track for discovering the life and power of the Word of God and the joy of having the constant relationship with a *know-it-all* God, the Holy Spirit.

Every day, I start by receiving "this is the day" as a good and perfect gift, knowing that another day was not promised. Each day is numbered, customized, packaged, and gifted to me. (Psalm 90:12). Every day, I look for God's expression of love to me, which then orders my day and includes the opportunity for me to express love to others: family, friends, community, and throughout all the Father has planned for me "this day."

Main Point:

Each day is a gift. As I unwrap the mystery of "this is the day" using the Word of God, I am totally connected to God.

Wise Woman

"Every wise woman buildeth her house:
but the foolish plucketh it down with her hands." —Proverbs 14:1

A wise Helper can grow into her office far beyond her normal human capacity. A wise woman is connected to God's Holy Spirit and postured to help in a supernatural state where needed. A wise Helper goes into her office using wisdom and faith as her hall pass.

It is very important that Eve is not seen as an *airhead* or a weak woman. Education is an enhancer, but it does not replace or compare to a wise woman who knows her office. I saw an interesting quote that came close to summing up a Helper's mantle. So, I enhanced it a bit. It read, "I can do anything, but I cannot do everything." Here is my enhancement:

> "I can do anything that I have been assigned to do. My primary resource is God, Holy Spirit, and my obedience to Him, and this is what prevents me from doing everything."

This sums up the Helper disposition of Eve quite well. I can do anything, but if I go for everything I can do, I will literally help myself to death! A Helper can get in the way of God, Holy Spirit, our Chief Helper, and strategist. I remember really making a mess out of a situation that did not have to be a mess. I cried out to the Lord for help, and I was so upset with myself. A loving calm came over me, and I realized I was learning and just because I know something, I should not want to go ahead of God, the Divine Helper.

An unwise Helper can help herself sick. Her actions literally allow her to embrace the curse. Few people consider the high rate of bodily sickness and disease that exists within the Helper population. In scripture, Miriam, who was Moses' and Aaron's sister, overstepped the guardrails, using her words to defame her brother's choice for his wife. She was cursed with leprosy. God slowed her down, but then He cleaned her up and restored her.

Know that being married is a lifelong assignment. However, it changes with the death of a spouse. It is a portrait of the work for a Helper. A Helper's capacity can include many assignments as the landscape of the household expands and grows, contracts, and then spills into legacy planning. It is not seasonal work. Much of it is learning as you live. The wise woman must sit with Holy Spirit in prayer regarding family, neighbors, church fellowship, and her job. The knowledge and understanding of biblical characters can be used to remind God of what He said and did by praying His Word. Build your wisdom. More importantly, we remind ourselves of the miracle-working power of God and His "just-in-time" interventions. Through this, by faith, we can execute and leverage His Words.

Let's review how God breaks out the attributes of this office. Primarily, Proverbs 31:10-31 is a good depiction of a wise Helper.

"A wife of noble character who can find?" (Proverbs 31:10 NIV). She cannot be found. She is appointed to Adam or Christ and His many projects within the Kingdom of God. The following reflects her basics.

She is a woman of prayer. As Eve masters her assignment to Adam by faith, she grows in her capacity to help Adam as his sphere increases. She can have children, plan and manage the household, and train younger women. She can develop businesses that can operate within Adams's sphere. She is loving, fit, holy, and looks good. In Proverbs 31, God describes in more detail the many qualities within the Office of Eve.

Eve, the human Helper, could be seen as a loyal wife, mother, and sister within the community. However, these qualities are a partial view of her assignments. She has the energy (health) of a prospering soul. (III John 1:2). Everywhere she goes and everything she does relates to planting good and harvesting good.

She operates in the love and righteousness of God. All females are born Helpers. However, Eve goes to her office using wisdom and faith, fully aware of her benefit package from God the Father. Eve is a wise woman.

The following discussion in the Book of Proverbs is about a wise woman. Helper attributes run through any line of work; however, the following are categories that can go wide based on the assignment and the degree of wisdom that is at work.

Note that the Helper depicted in the Book of Proverbs, Chapter 31, is a wise woman. The account of the woman in this passage makes it clear that she operates from the strength, intelligence, and Love of God through the restoration power of Jesus the Christ. Her supernatural abilities clearly point us to that conclusion. Like Jesus, she is a problem solver, operating out of *Love* and *Truth*. And like Jesus, she sees more than she speaks. She chooses her words carefully with a faith language that brings life, healing, and hope.

Then Jesus sent Holy Spirit to help. Holy Spirit, the Helper of God, then prescribes His help uniquely for each of us. Consideration for help is set up differently for a human Helper (a daughter of God) than an Adam (a son of God).

Main Point:

Eve is a wise woman, supernaturally infused by God, Holy Spirit.

In the Kingdom of God, there is a supernatural grid that empowers all citizens in the Kingdom who wish to participate. Wise women are plugged in. Their day-to-day assignments are connected to this grid and are lit up on demand. This supernatural grid provides strength and power to get extraordinary missions accomplished in an orderly and timely manner.

Remember, once you accepted and received Christ into your heart, the bridge that leads to God the Father was made possible because you believed. Your ability to believe was based on a supernatural infusion of faith gifted to every sinner so they can believe and receive salvation. Typical of our loving God, He always gives us what we need in order to do what we need to do to please Him.

This is the foundation for life in the Kingdom of God. All of this is what grows our faith as God's children. Faith in God and His Word is the path that leads to the Office of Eve. Faith is the door to the supernatural, fully available to Eve as her soul prospers. (III John 1:2). Ask Sarah, Abraham's wife, the Virgin Mary or her cousin, Elisabeth, who was John the Baptist's mother. Their stories are documented in scripture to show us that the signs and wonders of God are displayed through His children. (Isaiah 8:18).

The gift of faith helps us embrace our spirit life. There has been little recognition of that loving part of you. You have eyes that see, ears that hear, and thoughts that connect to your physical body. The Word of God puts all this in order: spirit, soul (mind), and body. Life is God's intention. This invites God's full presence into our whole life. Life without God leaves us living without the full presence of God, which nets out to the physical, ungodly world of Adam and Eve. When these two disobeyed God, their sin of disobedience killed (disconnected) our access to God. We have life in the physical, but our spirit life is disconnected. Access to God only comes in spirit and truth. This is Holy Spirit. His Word given is scripture. Scripture takes us to that truth. As we grow, it becomes very believable. As we believe, our mind gets properly reconnected to our sprit and then to the physical.

· As we grow in faith, through the Word of God, we will get to the point where we will not want to move without an instruction from The Holy. This protected growth area is what scriptures refer to as "a prospering soul." (III John 1:2). Everything changes when God's kingdom comes into our lives. As we know His love and His Word, we realize *if God said it, I believe it, and it is so.* As we begin to see the promises, benefits, and favor, we see The Way, which is the path Jesus has laid for each of us to go and become successful in living for God. God's Love becomes believable, not because it is something we can do. Rather, it is believable because He made a way for us to believe the unbelievable and receive these amazing gifts. As we grow in our faith, we become more confident in Him. His assuring and gentle Words, like those in Matthew 6:28-29 (NIV), "And why do you worry about clothes? See how the flowers of the field grow. They do not labor or spin. Yet I tell you that not even Solomon in all his splendor was dressed like one of these." He cares so much more for us, His children.

This is life on the Holy grid in the Kingdom of God. Eve, in her office, is connected to the power of God, The Holy. So believable.

Now, we can have the correct set of eyes to see the Proverbs 31 woman, who operates plugged in to the supernatural grid, which brings glory to God without a reward or attention to herself. You cannot be like her without the wisdom and strength that is connected to the supernatural grid powered by God the Father.

For your review, Proverbs 31, is listed in Extra Help for Helpers (C) The Proverbs 31 Woman in the rear of this book. As you read, you will notice the absence of today's depiction of superheroes and their powers. You will see how subtly this Helper moves in, through, and out of situations to complete her work. With love, she receives the plan and can see far beyond the natural in her work.

Wise Woman Disposition

1. She reflects the first commandment, which is where life starts, with Love. Her position is, *Because God loves me; I can show love to everyone in everything I do.* This includes *tough* love.

2. She reports to God, Holy Spirit, Chief Helper and Head of the Division of Help, Comfort and Joy.

3. She knows that wisdom from God is available for her to receive because she asked for it. (James 1:5).

4. She is assigned to an Adam and, as a result, is assigned to motherhood.

5. Because she understands her assignments, she can honor Adam by loving God and herself first. (Matthew 22:37-40). Not narcissistically, but to *do God.*

6. She displays holy restraint. Just because she knows, does not mean she speaks or acts.

7. She puts Adam and his household first, always.

8. She recognizes that being married to Christ is an honor, which is the training ground for a future assignment to an Adam.

9. She has the capacity for additional assignments, many of which are short-term and unplanned assignments.

10. She honors Adam as God honors Adam.

11. She saves and plans for scarce times.

12. She is a problem solver; she anticipates things.

13. She is appreciated by her husband and children. She plants the faith legacy.

14. She is protected by her husband (he is on watch at the city gates).

15. Her subconscious is reprogrammed by The Holy.

16. She looks for God-ordained sacrificial opportunities (gifts of Help).

17. Her prayer posture is organized and structured for communication with God morning, noon, and night. She participates in prayer meetings, prayer circles, and prayer partners. Her soul is restored.

18. She always looks good. She is more loving and beautiful with age.

Helper Benefit Package

For Helpers, God has cloaked their nature with an awesome Benefit Package, by faith. It is designed to address all the needs of a Helper so she can focus on her assignment and not her needs. Her nature and gentle use of power and strength often go unnoticed.

Benefit	Why this so good	Scripture Ref
Forgiven of all my iniquities (all sins, wrongdoings, and trespasses)		Psalm 103:3
Forgiveness	A constant forgiving of sins, which keeps us connected to God, through Jesus.	Matthew 6:12
Righteous	Death to sin; alive unto righteousness.	II Corinthians 5:21
Faith	A growth track through daily living and love.	Galatians 5:6
Comfort	Security, safety, the good.	Psalm 91:10
Customized Assignments	A work that is perfect for you. You can be a wife, a mom, an educator, or an artist, or all of these.	Jeremiah 29:11
God's Wisdom	Extra capacity to do more as assigned, available to God's children who ask for it.	James 1:5
God heals all my diseases		Psalm 103:3
Health	Prospering soul (not spirit)	III John 2:1
	Strength	Psalm 28:7
	Long Life	Psalm 91:16
God redeemed my life from destruction		Psalm 103:4
Good life	120-year health plan	Genesis 6:3
	Eternal life	Exodus 23:26
	Love	John 3:16
Jesus as The Way	Jesus—salvation and eternal life	John 14:6
	For my yoke is easy, and my burden is light.	Matthew 11:30
Protection	Full Armor	Ephesians 6:11
	Deliverance from evil	Matthew 6:13
	Angels to surround you	Psalm 91:11
God crowns me with lovingkindness and tender mercies		Psalm 103:4
Food and Water	Your daily bread: spiritual and physical nutrients	Exodus 23:25
		Matthew 6:11

All items within this package are supernaturally charged with the power of God through His Word and exercised by faith. God loves you so much that He built all this into His plan for you. (Jeremiah 29:11).

It is key to see that with all of Eve's endeavors, Adam or Christ are fully engaged. His sitting at the gate, as mentioned in Proverbs 31:23, indicates that he watches over Eve's coming and going and knows all the merchants (strong men), which allows her to do business and move about without harm. He is the chief of security for his household.

> **Main Point:**
>
> God loves you so much that He built benefits into His plan for you. (Jeremiah 29:11).

Short Stories of Helpers and Eves

Since the foundation of the earth, women have had key roles as Helpers in miracles and life situations highlighted throughout scripture. The non-loving situations some of them found themselves in depict for us the constant attempt by the devil to destroy the works of God and have his way with Helpers, even until today. These stories all include an experience where the divine hand of God assisted them. It also happened in my life.

This story is about an Eve; she was my father's mother. I never knew her. My dad never knew her. I know, however, that she fell into hard times.

She obeyed God by not aborting him, and not killing herself. Instead, shortly after his birth, she placed him on the steps of a New York City hospital, where he would be found and cared for. She was most likely able to watch her baby's discovery, like Moses' sister, who watched him drift down the river in a basket, to see him be found and taken in.

My life and seven other children are my father's seed with promise. God saw me before Dad was born and all throughout his challenging childhood as an orphan. Dad gave his life to Christ and found hope and a future. He was given a beautiful woman to marry, and she brought forth eight children.

In other words, my dad was abandoned as a newborn infant, wrapped in a blanket, and laid on the steps of a hospital. His mother knew that caring people inside the hospital would give this little king of Color (in the year 1921) the opportunity for the life he deserved, which she could not do for him.

The following Helper stories found in scripture describe Helpers who stayed the course. We see God handle the impossible. We see faith activated, supernatural events taking place, and Helpers operating within the Office of Eve.

Some Helpers were not given a name or natural origin in scripture. They could have been angels *unawares*, as mentioned in Hebrews 13:2, "Be not forgetful to entertain strangers: for thereby some have entertained angels unawares."

Angels are from the Helper division of heaven. Under Holy Spirit's leadership, they are assigned to whomever or whatever task is needed. They remain available today as we pray God's Word in situations. Angels only respond to God's Word.

Anna — a prophetess having eyes that saw and ears that heard. She was assigned an Adam for seven years and then entered widowhood. God has a special place in His heart for Helpers who lose their assignment to an Adam. He looks after them, giving them a season to become whole again. Anna was the daughter of Phanuel of the Tribe of Asher (son of Jacob), and she was a constant prayer warrior in the temple. Anna validated the Christ child. (Luke 2:36).

Deborah — appointed judge for the people of Israel, prophetess, and wife. She gave a message from God to Barak to go to war. She accompanied Barak in battle and successfully delivered Israel from the hand of Sisera, in the land of Harosheth of the Gentiles. (Judges 4:4).

Dorcas (Tabitha) — married to Christ, community worker, and seamstress. Her death was untimely. She was raised from the dead by Peter, which demonstrated the power in the Name of Jesus Christ. (Acts 9:36).

Esther — masterfully used her Eve office as queen to save her people during an ethnic cleansing attempt. She then established communities and a culture for God's people. (The Book of Esther).

Elisabeth — wife of a priest named Zacharias. She was barren, but was then blessed to give birth in her old age. She was the mother of John the Baptist, and cousin of the Virgin Mary. (Luke 1:24, 36).

Hagar — an Egyptian employee in the household of Abraham. In Sarah's attempt to help God out with the promise of a son, she assigned Hagar to become a surrogate mother for her. Abraham married her and Hagar bore a son (Ishmael) to Abraham. That was not God's plan. Sarah had her removed from Abraham's household. In her wilderness state, Hagar received a special visit from God, and was divinely provided for when she was homeless, while being a *single mom*. (Genesis 16:15).

Hannah — The wife of Elkanah, a woman with a sorrowful spirit and barren, for the Lord had shut up her womb. In prayer at the temple with Eli the priest being present, she made a vow to God that if He would grant her a son, she will give him unto the Lord, and his hair would never be cut. God granted her a son and after weaning, she turned him over to Eli at the temple. The child's name is Samuel, who became an anointed prophet within Israel. God used him to appoint Saul and David as king. (I Samuel 1:1-15).

Jochebed — a daughter of Levi. She kept her baby boy, Moses, alive at a time when midwives were instructed to kill all the Hebrew male babies at birth. She saved her son, which was against Egyptian law. God had big plans for this man-child. She was also the mother of Aaron and Miriam. (Numbers 26:59).

Keturah — assigned as wife to Abraham after Sarah died. She bore several sons to Abraham, but these were not a part of the covenant. They were blessed by Abraham. (Genesis 25:1).

Mary — the mother of Jesus (the virgin birth), triggered the wine miracle at the wedding, which was the first miracle performed by Jesus. She used her faith to become the mother of Jesus, Son of Man, Son of God.

Mary pondered, watched and witnessed Jesus grow up into the Savior. (Luke 2:19). From birth to the cross and resurrection, there was Mary. Her faith in God's message from the holy angel infused each reality as this truth unfolded. Her personal prayer life, meditation time, and many situations allowed her faith to wax strong in her God throughout Jesus' life on earth. Jesus, as a child, was potentially a handful. As a human child, He did not skip steps in His development. God was there to assist in raising Jesus, just like He is with us in raising our children. Mary was also in place at the cross. (Luke 1:27, John 2:1, John 19:25-26).

Mary and Elisabeth — gifted cousins who fellowshipped and worshipped God together. At Mary's visit, Elisabeth received a special dispensation of the Holy Spirit of God in her womb, which reinforced the realm of miracles they were in: a virgin conception, who would be Jesus and an old-age conception and birth, who would be John the Baptist. (Luke 1).

Mary and Martha — sisters of Lazarus. Lazarus, Mary, and Martha befriended Jesus; they were like family. They were chosen. Scripture highlights the contrast between their gifts and spiritual maturity. Mary chose to sit at Jesus' feet for learning, while Martha was more caring and hospitable. (John 11:1).

Miriam — Moses' and Aaron's sister. She watched over her baby brother, Moses, as he floated downstream in a basket and was retrieved by Pharaoh's daughter. Miriam had a leadership role (among the women) with Moses and Aaron during the trip through the wilderness. She spoke in an out-of-control manner against Moses and his Ethiopian wife. God struck her with leprosy, which then placed her outside of the camp. Then, God delivered her. (Numbers 26:59, Micah 6:4).

(The) **Poor widow** — a widow who decided to sow a seed using her last two cents and give it to God. Jesus observed her offering and the offering of others who gave out of their wealth. Jesus realized this widow gave her all, out of her lack, and He counted it worth far more than the others, noting she had given more than all the wealthy givers who gave a lot, but not everything, as this widow did. (Mark 12:42).

Rahab — her home was strategically placed right at Jericho's wall. She hid the Hebrew spies sent by Joshua and received God's favor, saving her household. (Hebrews 11:31).

Rebekah — a virgin assigned to Isaac. Blessed and chosen. Isaac took her to Sarah's tent, where the blessing was. She bore twins named Jacob and Esau. (Genesis 25:21-26).

Ruth — a Moabite, young and widowed. She loved and cared for her mother-in-law, Naomi, who was also widowed. She returned home with Naomi after accepting Naomi's God of the people of Israel. She entered the lineage of Jesus by marrying Boaz, a man of honor and wealth in Bethlehem. (Ruth 1).

Sarah — loved God and highly honored her husband (Abraham) and his faith. She was blessed with an *old age* birth, which brought forth the promised son, Isaac. Stunningly beautiful, strong in faith,

she was mentioned in the New Testament for honoring her Adam. "…
You'll be true daughters of Sarah if you do the same, unanxious and
unintimidated." (I Peter 3:5-6 MSG).

Shiphrah — a Hebrew midwife who refused to obey the order of
Pharoah to kill the Hebrew male infants. (Exodus 1:15).

(The) **Shunammite woman** — given a child, as she and her
husband cared for the prophet. Her man-child died. She received the
blessing from her husband to *go* to the man of God for help. Her son
was restored to life by the prophet Elisha. (II Kings 4:8-12).

Wife of Pontius Pilot — intervened in the sentencing of Jesus.
At the inquisition of Jesus by the Jewish mob, Pilot's wife sent him a
message saying, "Have thou nothing to do with that just man: for I have
suffered many things this day in a dream because of him." This was her
attempt to prevent her husband from harming Jesus. (Matthew 27:19).

Women at the tomb — faithful followers of Jesus. Some of the
women who witnessed Jesus' death could not let Him be laid to rest
unattended, so they gathered sweet spices and set out to anoint His
body. As they went, they thought of the big stone that sealed the tomb,
and they wondered who would roll it away for them. But by faith,
they continued on, and when they arrived, the stone had already been
removed. They met an angel, a holy Helper, who spoke comfort and
joy about the risen Savior, telling them there was no body to anoint
because Jesus had already risen. The angel told these women to, "Go
your way…" and carry the message of Jesus' resurrection to Peter and
the disciples. An interesting observation here is that in this passage of
scripture, we see that Helpers (angels and human) were first to deliver
this good news! (Mark 16:1-7).

> **Main Point:**
>
> The stories above all include an experience where the divine hand of God assisted the women.

Helpers Who are Leaders

Married Eves do not need to lead in the traditional sense. They do best with the big picture and operating at key points of an effort. They help leaders in good and powerful ways. However, Eves are also capable of leading when assigned. It is important to note that a Helper does not lead in the same manner that male leaders operate. She uses her position and power gently and in targeted ways.

She must see it as an assignment and know when to pull back or get out of a situation. God, Holy Spirit (the *Assigner*), will show her the way out of the role when her assignment is done. A Helper in a leadership role must stay connected to keep the assignment clear. In this way, she will know when her part is completed.

It is not your way; it is God's way and will for you. For example, you may think there is more to be done. However, that work could be for someone else to do. But if you do not move when told, you are now in the way and out of order. There will be carrots and shiny objects set up to keep you distracted and from obeying God. Simply ask Holy Spirit to lead you out of this role and you can move on to your next assignment.

A good example in scripture is Deborah, an appointed judge for the people of Israel, a prophetess, and a wife. She gave a message from God to go to war. She accompanied Barak (an army chief) in battle at his request and successfully delivered Israel from the hand of Sisera, in the land of Harosheth of the Gentiles. (Judges 4:4). In Deborah's efforts to help God's people, other women in the Helper community, like Ja'-el, rose with the wisdom and power of Eve to become part of the war strategy. Ja'-el, Heber's wife, was given the opportunity to kill Sisera the captain of the enemy army. When God did this for Israel, Deborah praised God, pulled out and the land had rest for forty years. (Judges 5).

Helpers can flow in and out of assignments. Deborah and Ja'-el continued to be wives. Helpers in Christ have the extra capacity to take on assignments where help is needed.

Helpers from All Ethnic Origins

Christ demonstrated His love for Helpers in the account of His visit with the woman at the well in Samaria. (John 4:6-39). It was a planned work of the Father. Jesus announced to His disciples that He needed to go to Samaria. In doing this, Jesus interacted across cultural, racial, and gender lines. This woman had already had five husbands (forms of Adam), plus at least one other.

She did not tell Jesus these things. Jesus told *her* about her life and offered her eternal life. That encounter with Jesus brought forth her salvation and deliverance. Christ restored her to Eve status. Her Helper nature, cleansed by the Blood of Jesus, kicked in and she used her Eve office to spread the good news of Christ.

Widows

Widowhood (Adam dies) is a transition in which a Helper becomes reconnected in marriage to Christ. Other than the great divorce of Queen Vashti from King Ahasuerus (Xerxes), marriages highlighted in scripture are broken only by death. When Adam dies, the oneness is broken. Unlike other deaths, the entire family experiences a bereavement season. Eve has this bereavement, but she also enters widowhood. In widowhood, a widow must embrace the everyday situations that remain, spiritually encircle her Adam's estate, and immediately give it to God for a hedge of protection. God will then carve out a new normal. This is the time when the oneness God gave the two is severed, and the Helper gets a new attachment to Christ. God moves in very close to oversee life for this Helper on the other side of the Adam assignment.

Widows are Helpers set aside for healing, repair, and restoration to Christ. In the book of wisdom, it states that "She will do him good and not evil all the days of her life." (Proverbs 31:12). It appears that Helpers are expected to outlive their Adams. She will need direction on how to close Adam's household and territory, or settle his estate. Ask God for the wisdom to live in widowhood perfectly. There is not a timeframe for this process, as it is customized daily for each Helper.

After the healing, Eve can be assigned to another work. Proclaim that you have eyes to see and ears to hear. Seek God's will and ask Holy Spirit for help. There may also be wise counsel from Eves within the Helper community.

In scripture we clearly see the love God has for widows and the wisdom He gives to them. We see in the Book of Ruth how God lovingly and supernaturally navigated Ruth and her mother-in-law, Naomi, to a blessed survivorship. (Ruth 1).

One story overlooked by many tells of how Jesus, while living here on earth as the eldest son, cared for His mother, Mary. She was with Him before ministry and during ministry. She was not looking after her adult son; her adult son was looking after His widowed mother. This became more evident at the cross when Jesus assigned Mary to one of the disciples. (John 19:26). This was a powerful display of love, showing us that even during His departure, Jesus left His earthly relationships in order, as a good Adam, son of God, would do.

One can see, by faith, that Jesus has a special place in His heart for this special Helper — a widow. Widowhood is not to be wasted. The affection from Christ to Eve, support from her church fellowship, family, and the Helper community, is invaluable. It is the path to becoming whole again. The disciples received a clear indication of this in Acts 6:1.

I must share this story. I was on a medical missionary journey to Southern Africa. One of my roommates was a widow who shared that she had enjoyed a wonderful marriage and had a difficult time letting it all go. She said one day, she prayed to the Father for Him to show her what it was that He wanted her to do — something she could not do if her husband was still alive. Then, the opportunity to lead a national organization of Christian educators appeared, including starting a school in Zambia. She has great memories of her life with her husband, and now she sees her value to God and views her new assignment with joy!

Wise Helpers understand the scripture that calls her a *daughter* of Sarah. (I Peter 3:6). Sarah not only loved Abraham, but more importantly, she honored him. If you can honor the Father's attachment (you to Adam) as a good and perfect gift, it is not a surprise then, that if the gift is removed, the Father will move into your heart with what is needed to make you whole. Adam leaving is not personal. God's role in this process is very personal, all-loving, and good.

One other story in scripture we should discuss is found in I Samuel 25:2-3, 18-41. Abigail was a woman of great understanding and had a beautiful countenance. She was a wise Helper and married to Nabal, a very wealthy, but evil man. His operations included a territory located next to David's camp. David made sure to respect Nabal's territory. Nabal's men knew that a wall of protection and peace was with them by being close to God's presence with David.

Nabal was beyond disrespectful in behavior and unappreciative in his attitude toward David. Abigail heard about it and moved quickly to correct Nabal's foolish mistake, bringing provisions to David and his men and pleading for the lives of her husband and his household. She saw her husband stand against the God of Israel. Her people knew about the Red Sea miracle, the Jericho wall miracle, Saul's reign and fall, and now David's leadership. Her kind, quick act saved them all. However, her husband Nabal self-destructed and died a few days later. Then, she was an unprotected widow. David had Abigail brought to him and covered her by marrying her. I see this as symbolic of how God moves, having Helpers marry Christ as their covering during widowhood and beyond.

Helper, Detached From God

A Helper who is detached from God is (with her skills), working against God and herself. Satan has deceived her into thinking that she is okay and does not need a leader. We see throughout the Bible that Helpers need godly leadership.

A Helper who is independent of Christ is a survivor and will seek to control her life, being the boss and ruler of her life. She can be dysfunctional, like a lid blowing steam from a pressure cooker. She is *OFF!* She takes charge because *it* must get done! It sets her off when there is a lack of progress *her* way. She proclaims, "How can we ever get anything done? I will do it myself." This woman wonders why God made men, who are mostly in her way. She feels she will just have to work around or mow over them.

In the Book of Esther, we see firsthand how God dealt with a Helper who was not wise. Queen Vashti was summoned to help the king entertain his guests. A wise woman commits to do her Adam good and not evil all the days of her life. (Proverbs 31:12). Personal sacrifice is a key attribute of a wise Helper. She was not asked to dance or do anything but be the king's most prized possession and display her royal beauty. But this day, she brought him much embarrassment throughout the entire kingdom. (Esther 1:9-12).

God prefers not to use a Helper who is not in her office, regardless of her earthly position. The divorce of Queen Vashti from King Ahasuerus (Xerxes) is the only broken marriage I see in scripture, other than by death. Even with this Helper offense, God did not allow harm to come to her.

As girls watch these Helpers (who are detached from Jesus) follow this path, many become women who are annoyed, critical or screamers (audibly or internally). Their sons watch and become confused, wanting to be Helpers or grow up to destroy them. Under a dysfunctional Helper, some boys may grow up planting violence with their seed, breeding evil and destruction.

She unknowingly uses her gifts, talents, and education to dethrone Adam. A Helper makes a mess when she oversteps her role to control and correct. This causes damage to the marriage relationship. Satan continues to use her to belittle and weaken Adam by creating loneliness, confusion, or an identity crisis. Now, she desires the power to be equal, to become a teacher or leader of men, president or king, leading entire populations of men.

Without Christ, a Helper is in a confused state. She is powerful, but in an unprotected sense. She is dangerous; she can be used to do good without the truth, having potential assignments from God, but living outside of the Kingdom of God. She is in danger because she has no hedge of protection against the kingdom of darkness. A Helper without God is vulnerable to satanic attacks and agendas that keep her from reaching for Jesus, the Savior. She can be tricked again and again. Even though she is not in Christ, she continues to help because it is in her nature to help, for good or not for good.

Without Christ, an ungodly Helper is feminine, seductive, and focused on what she desires. She works her plan and has Satan's help to accomplish it. Her goal could be to take someone's marriage, a man or woman, power, a job, or any earthly possession. (Proverbs 7:5).

Main Point:

Without Christ, a Helper is in a confused state. She is powerful, but in an unprotected sense.

Life With God Must Be Restored

"For God so loved the world, that he gave his only begotten Son,
that whosoever believeth in him should not perish,
but have everlasting life." —John 3:16

It is important to remember that Christ's birth, death, and resurrection restored God's intentions for us. The Office of Adam and The Office of Eve were restored. Jesus assumed our sin and wrong decisions. Christ was crucified to death. It was not just a nail or two into his flesh, but He hung on the cross with all the sin, sickness, and disease of the entire world (including yours and mine) for all time, on His body. He died this way. He rose from the dead, bringing back the original plan of God.

Satan established sinful strongholds (culture) in the world that cause the plan of redemption to be more essential to our survival. Eve was deceived by Satan. Jesus is The Way, The Truth, and The Life to all who will receive Him. (John 14:6). This redemption plan (what Jesus did), is the only way back to God the Father.

This redemption offer is not forced upon us; we get to make the choice. You can live your entire earth-realm life without Christ. But the end game is that you will have to live in hell with Satan. These are not my words, but the Word of God. (Revelation 20:15). Because your soul never dies, there is a lot more living to do than just here in this earth realm. We were all born to live forever, somewhere. So, we need to hook up with Christ now, before we get to our next life.

The deceiver of Eve is also after you. As wonderful as life appears, not planning for your next life will be the ultimate successful plan of the deceiver. The deceiver's strategy for your life is to have you destroy yourself or position you to destroy as many others as possible along your way to self-destruction. This will not end happily. (Romans 6:23).

It is not about going to church, holding great positions in your community, or even doing good. These works are all fine, however, good deeds *cannot* save your soul. Most important, it *is* about saving your *soul,* the part of you that never dies. By accepting Christ, you can now live the good life forever based on what Christ Jesus arranged and gifted just for you. It is *being protected while you are here* (doing those good works), and then being able to spend your next life in love and at peace with God the Father.

Being protected while you are here should be noted as one of the many benefits of salvation. In the spirit realm, children of God, through Christ, have a banner over them indicating they belong to Him. This means any spiritual violation must first get the *okay* from Jesus, which is not going to happen. In Christ, no curse, fiery dart, or other weapon can profit by attacking you. You are covered from any attempt of the deceiver against you. Weapons may be formed against you, but God's Word promises that no weapon that is formed against you can prosper. (Isaiah 54:17).

Holy Spirit, the Chief Helper, has attached a wire (called *faith*) to you to help you come to Christ now. If you have not yet accepted Christ as your Lord and Savior, go to Extra Help for Helpers (A) Connect to

Christ, to accept the invitation and receive your new life in Christ! Then, please come back to the following section entitled, "**Now that you have Christ in your life**."

*   *   *   *   *

Now that you have Christ in your life.

A party has taken place in heaven for you! No joke! We celebrate with you and pray for your Christian journey. (Luke 15:10).

Walking with Christ.

Your handheld device with the Bible App is good, however your ability to have the Word of God available should not be dependent upon the electrical grid within your community. The Bible is the Word of God. It will be helpful for you to own a Bible. The Word of God is living and by the faith within you, you must begin to see that if God said it, that is it! Let's talk about the *new* you!

Be the *new* you.

You are new! (II Corinthians 5:17). Know that for many of us, we are already operating in our assignments. However, what is new is a clear set of eyes that allows you to view and value that assignment differently. Others of us realize that in this new life, the situation we are in is *not* lining up with the love and the enormous potential of our new life in Christ. Ask Holy Spirit to lead you out of that situation.

Receive these gifts from God now!

<u>Righteousness</u>: God is totally holy. You can never measure up to God. Jesus makes us righteous. (Romans 6:18). Now, there is no looking back on any sin or bad choices.

<u>Love</u>: So that you can believe and appreciate His plan for your life forever. (John 3:16). Love is needed so you can obey God's command

to love Him. (Matthew 22:37). He will teach you how to love Him, yourself, and others.

Protection: No fear, no confusion, and no evil. This is all in God's Word, the Bible. We must know what God says. A good start is Psalm 91 and Ephesians 6:10.

Make this work. These are the things that will help you in your new life in Christ:

New Belief System:

> Understand and believe in the Love of God and the Love of Jesus Christ.

New Habits (for your new life):

> Daily exercises
> Praise and prayer
> Scripture reading
> Affirmations
> Expect miracles every day

New Relationships:

> Church
> Worship
> Fellowship, ministry, projects
> Family, newness of Love (new source of loving)

Build Your Faith:

> Keys to the Kingdom
> Prospering soul – good health
> Wisdom of God, from God
> Say what God says. Copy Him.

Ask to become aware of your assignment. (*See* Prayer for The Wisdom of God in Prayer Toolkit.)

Know your Benefit Package and use it. (*See* Helper Benefit Package.)

Remember that your life starts in truth with Jesus and by faith in the spirit realm with God the Father.

CHAPTER 4

Helper Parenting

- Helpers Who Have Sons
- Helpers Who Have Daughters
- The Fence – Hedge of Protection
- A Mother's (Helper's) Reach
- Single Mom
- Checklist for Helpers with Children

Helper Parenting

Parents must have a presence wherever their children are. Even when you are not with them, make it so that whenever someone sees your child, they envision your face (presence and as protector) over the child. This makes them all accountable for their actions and helps them understand permitted behaviors.

Children under God have a special connection to Him and His plan. To Adam, He grants favor to his household. God describes Adam's children as offshoots or olive plants springing from Eve, the fruitful vine, to establish the legacy of godliness and service. (Psalm 128:3).

Motherhood out of the Office of Eve is primarily a prayer posture for wisdom to follow Holy Spirit's lead. It is not conscious, but an innate deposit made at the beginning of motherhood.

A mother is a mom because she has been empowered by God to grow a baby and then discharge it out of the womb and into her world at the perfect time. She suffered (lived) the supernatural development and bore witness to the uniqueness and greatness of the child.

Children are born not fully developed. They have less cognitive ability, as the brain continues to develop for about twenty years. They need protection and loving care. During this time, a child moves in and out of situations of excellent mental clarity, to thoughts and decisions that make no sense. Mothers have the love for that child to keep them safe, sound, and strong in spirit, mind, and body. She protects their world and respects the innocence that has been assigned to her.

A mother knows the potential in a child and is set to nurture the seed within them for great accomplishments. A mother who lacks must move along in faith to plant the legacy. Mothers who do not lack must move along in faith to plant the legacy, by teaching what is most important, not allowing things to cloud the way.

Helpers Who Have Sons

"Thy wife shall be as a fruitful vine by the sides of thine house: thy children like olive plants round about thy table." —Psalm 128:3.

With baby sons, a Helper will lean heavily upon Holy Spirit's guidance. It is very different raising a son (a king) versus raising a daughter (a Helper).

The love, discipline, character, and examples play out differently. Sons of God are leaders in training. They must be raised with their future leadership role respected and harnessed using discipline and tough work. They must become strong, responsible and of good character. If there is an Adam, help him raise this son. If there is no physical Adam, you will be led by Christ as to how and when, and who, is to help shape this young man.

If your son is older and does not believe Christ as his Lord, Savior, and elder brother, then this is where you begin your prayer for his salvation and God's hedge of protection as outlined in Psalm 91. Understand that you and God, Holy Spirit, unite, as the Helper petitioning the Chief Helper for help with your son. As Helper, you are slow to speak and quick to hear Holy Spirit's lead. You do not have an opinion to offer, only if wisdom makes it clear and in order. Jesus' mother would have changed the story in John 2:8, at the wedding had she been highly opinionated.

The Book of Proverbs is the book of wisdom, and it outlines the characteristics of a wise person. It also tells how to avoid evil, traps, and fools. In Chapter 31, the message from King Lemuel's mother addresses two areas for kings to understand and use self-control: strange women and drinking, both lead to intoxication. Watch your words and use your role as Eve wisely. With adult sons, it is not your role to correct or teach. Ask Holy Spirit to correct and teach you and him, specifically as issues arise. As mom, you get a front row seat to see what you have shaped when you were rearing him. What you should observe is a collection of values and emotions, good ones, and untapped ones. No emotions are bad, some are just more regulated and lifegiving than others. Like Mary, you may ask him questions or make a statement that triggers his own thoughts and solutions. (John 2:3-5).

In Proverbs 31, King Lemuel's mother starts this passage by establishing her position and her right as a mother. She states that because she gave birth to him; she has maintained that spiritual connection, understanding of him and his vulnerabilities. The Bible has recorded few instances where women (Helpers) are giving instruction to a man.

This prophetess Helper-mother is best qualified to give these words to her son but understands it is a rare opportunity. With wisdom, she is aware of how her family lineage could be impacted if her son got involved with an ungodly Helper, so she lightly addresses it. Then, in verses 10 through 31 describes for him the traits of a good woman and how he benefits. She wants her Helper nature to relate to his soon-to-be assigned Helper (wife). She suggests this is his "rite of passage" to the good life. She also addresses the use of alcohol and the impacts on the brain, memory, and disruptions to critical landmarks (belief systems) that ruin lives and could take a lifetime to recover from.

Begin praying for your son's Helper, who will be assigned to him. Pray for God's will, their preparation, and pray that they be kept from evil. Even if your son is a little boy, I recommend this prayer posture, so that by faith, the Love of God will be at work way in advance of that union.

Your words bear fruit, so use them cautiously.

Helpers Who Have Daughters

Helpers must teach little Helpers, according to Proverbs 31:28. Little girls will copy the women who are in their lives. She is taught mostly by example. Helpers must learn:

- the art of prayer and the role of a Helper in life.
- to stay closely attached to her leadership. A Helper needs to be protected until her Adam is presented. She must obey her parents and she must stick with Christ.
- to sow seeds of love, not hate, and to know the difference.
- to know the art of restraint and self-control; to see and decide.
- to avoid situations with boys and men that violate her personal space.
- to accept that life is full of assignments. Good habits, organization, and discipline; school, church school, volunteer work, sports, and clubs all have a Helper perspective to them.

- to understand that Holy Spirit needs Helpers to assign. There are no shortages. There are plenty of potential Adams and perfect assignments.
- to understand that she is not to look for an Adam, but pray in detail for him.

So, the mother of a girl child must seek to spiritually connect the "Holy Spirit Help to her daughter's Helper nature.

- A mother with an adult Helper daughter must be wise and in constant communication (prayer) for guidance in helping her daughter in life; keeping her whole, undistracted, protected, and pointed to Christ is key.
- Single women, meanwhile, must become Helpers married to Christ. He is your daughter's covering (including being her functional father if she has no father). Before her Adam arrives, she can practice restraint and learn to watch her words by using them to benefit the hearer. (Ephesians 4:29).

In the spirit realm, a single daughter has *Helper* written all over her. Now, her assignment is in Christ. Helpers always have an assignment, but if she is unaware of this, God's enemy will use her because she helps anybody if she does not understand her mission. The enemy of God is in full pursuit of an adult Helper. He knows her potential, even though she may not.

The Fence — Hedge of Protection

The secret ingredient for believers who have children is to build a fence around them, by faith, with the Holy Spirit of God. This Holy Spirit fence is a hedge of protection around your children.

Holy Spirit will do much more than you can do. He can filter what children hear and what they really see. For example, as much as you work at preventing ungodly exposure, there may be something your child is exposed to, like an inappropriate word, song, or image. It does not get absorbed or stored in their memory. Holy Spirit can control their dreams and thoughts. When your child is at school or out with friends, He can keep the child from evil and remain on watch for your child. Holy Spirit will keep you calm, reminding you of appropriate words from the Father.

We must remember that Jesus was born a baby, fully human, and went through every stage of childhood, including puberty!

I have seen no scripture that says Jesus was a mild-mannered child. You may recall an account in scripture where Jesus, at the age of twelve, did not stay with his family while traveling. When they found him, several days later, He was in the temple going toe-to-toe with the temple leaders. His response was not what they had expected. (Luke 2:44). He was a typical child, not a knucklehead, but not always considerate, just like any child. Mary and Joseph raised a very outgoing, free-spirited boy with the help of the fence (Holy Spirit).

Scripture also indicates that Jesus grew and became strong in spirit, was filled with wisdom, and the grace of God was upon Him. Luke 2:51 tells us He was subject to them, which shows He was learning to be respectful. We can pray:

> "I declare and decree Luke 2:40-51 over my child. Thank You that she shall grow and become strong in spirit, filled with wisdom, and the grace of God be upon her. This child is also subject to me. In Jesus' Name. Amen."

When a horse trainer receives a new, wild pony, it is basically untrained. The best thing to do until it calms down and feels safe and loved is to put the pony within a fence. It leaps and dances around and does not appreciate order. Over time, it calms down and can be trained.

You can declare that your child is in the fence, in Jesus' Name. Amen. This fence is Holy Spirit. Parents are the gatekeepers, and the angels of the Lord keep watch. With this, we can receive peace and not allow things to get out of hand. We can ask the Lord to keep them from evil (Matthew 6:13), to protect their thoughts and exposures, including all exposures from the prince of the power of the air, who is Satan. (Ephesians 2:2). God will protect their sleep, pick their friends, keep them from bullies, and give them a safe place to grow.

Holy Spirit-inflamed hedges of protection are invaluable for your children. You cannot be everywhere with them, but God is always there. In this fence, I can pray the Word of God over my child. Other times, because Holy Spirit and I have this understanding, I may only be able to say *"he or she is in the fence. In Jesus' Name,"* and I have executed the Word of God over them.

Adam is lord over his children. They must be taught to honor him, for it is a commandment with promise. Eve rears their children under the authority of Adam. Sometimes, she may even have to remind the children that their dad (Adam) will correct a behavior in them.

Meanwhile, Eve prays for the anointing and leadership needed to successfully rear his children as she realizes the responsibility he has. Our current culture dismisses the need for a father in the home. Therefore, many children will not grow up with the leadership of their Adam, at least not in the home. However, in a situation where there is no Adam present, the Helper nature of Eve kicks in. She plugs in to Jesus, her spiritual husband, and they lead. Marriage to Christ for leadership, provision, and wisdom as to how to rear children in their current environment is essential, allowing Eve to plant "the good" in the midst of every day.

Prayers must be prayed as soon as possible for this boy child or girl child, the vision, the help, and the plan. Pray at the start that their experience and exposure will be ordered in The Way to prepare for the work in each child.

A Mother's (Helper's) Reach

"There is a lad here, which hath five barley loaves, and two small fishes..." —John 6:9

Little is known about the lad with the five loaves and two fish in scripture. (Matthew 14:17). However, he *did* witness the teachings of Jesus. So, where do you get lunch in that situation? It was obviously something that someone who cared for him made sure he carried with him for the journey. It gives the appearance that there was a caring Helper, sending him off, providing him with his own care package. This group was following the teachings and the wondrous works of Jesus Christ.

If we were to look at the nutritional value of barley, a whole grain, and the protein, good fat, vitamins, and minerals in fish, we can see that it was a quality meal for travelers, giving energy and long-term sustenance for their journey. This meal was perfect for feeding a boy *and* a multitude. This story illustrates how Helpers help without looking for credit or recognition. Helpers do small acts (seedlike) that yield large-scale, life-changing benefits. The gentle power of an Eve is postured for signs and wonders.

Single Mom

Helpers who have children and no husband are very special human Helpers. Unfortunately, our society tends to look down on the Helper, and as a result, they suffer. For example, a single mom in scripture, named Hagar, maiden of Sarah, was given to Abraham to wife and to bear a son named Ishmael. (Genesis 16:1). Sarah, his wife, then became envious, and Hagar was forced out. She fell upon hard times, but God came to her aid.

It appears that being a single mom is a life of extreme sacrifice, pain, discomfort, but also joy. It cannot be compared to anything else except the sacrifice and unconditional love of Jesus. There is another biblical account of a loving single mom, which is found in I Kings 3:16-27. Two women had babies; one baby died. They began fighting over the one living baby, each claiming the child as her own. Using the wisdom of God, King Solomon ordered that the living child be cut in half, and each woman be given a portion of the child. However, before the order was carried out, the real mother made an immediate sacrifice and asked that the full living child be given to the other woman. Because of her love for her baby, she desired to keep the child alive. With that, Solomon knew, and he gave the child to its rightful mother.

God's grace is available for all single moms. His love does not consider their pedigree, the social-economic status, or under what conditions the child was conceived. It is a family, with Jesus as the head. In the absence of a father, God helps the mother to parent and helps the child develop and learn.

Saved Helpers (moms) see this wonder and are grateful. We must pray that the unsaved Helpers (moms) do not push God away from their situation and try to handle it on their own.

Checklist for Helpers with Children

There are some things critical to children that must be taught. The deceiver (Satan) will not want you to remember or have time to do these things. The busyness of life, reacting to evil attacks, and unplanned events, cause us to simply not have space to do the right things in the development of a child.

- Honor God and know who He is.
- Understand the power of prayer.
- Teach children to respect their parents and adults. Parents are not friends.
- Create or identify situations to teach children to make proper decisions and make positive choices.
- Teach children how to manage time.
- Use housework and sports for teamwork and development.
- Hold family meetings and Bible studies.

The Ten Commandments are always the perfect playbook for children, using situations and life's circumstances to apply. They help build character and Christlike values.

Helper Moving Toward Her Office

Helpers Who Overhelp (Suffer Death)

CHAPTER 5

✿

Helper Moving Toward Her Office

Helpers Who Overhelp (Suffer Death)

Because Helpers can develop solutions that help, it is always a point that true Helpers stay connected to God, Holy Spirit, to be sure their solutions are from Him. Helpers in Christ, or not in Christ, help.

One biblical account of Helpers overhelping is Sarah with her Adam, Abraham. (Genesis 16:1). God had told Abraham that he would be the father of many nations. Sarah decided, based on her age, bareness, and the time passed since God made the promise, that it was highly unlikely. So, she presented her maiden named Hagar to Abraham to wed and produce this promised child. A good human Helper idea, but not God's idea. Hagar produced a son named Ishmael. But God made it clear that he was not the promised son. Hagar ended up homeless and distraught, and Sarah and Abraham were still waiting on the promised son.

Throughout history, we see Helpers doing things that are beyond their assignment. They reach and do things that are not ordered by God. Helpers can unknowingly flow into God's *permissive* will and outside of His *perfect* will. In Proverbs, the book of wisdom, it states, "There is a way that seemeth right unto a man, but the end thereof are the ways of death." (Proverbs 16:25). A Helper must stay connected to the leadership of God to know her assignments and see the lines of her work drawn by God.

"Just because you can, does not mean you do." —Surina Ann Jordan, PhD

CHAPTER 6

Single Helpers

- Sex Outside of Marriage (Fornication)
- So Why Can't We Just Live Together?

CHAPTER 6

Single Helpers

"For thy Maker is thine husband; the LORD of hosts is his name;
and thy Redeemer the Holy One of Israel;
The God of the whole earth shall he be called." —Isaiah 54:5

"...The unmarried woman careth for the things of the Lord,
that she may be holy both in body and in spirit:" —I Corinthians 7:34

The unmarried Helper must be married to Christ. Because there is no earthly Adam assigned to her, she has a special intercessory role from God, Holy Spirit, for Christ's heart (will) and His Body, the Church. Know that God does not have to honor anyone between Himself and Eve unless she is married.

If a Helper is currently not assigned to an Adam... good! She should rejoice during this time and go to God for her "what next." An essential part of her *next* is accepting the call on her life to be an Eve (Helper). All things will shift and become easily ordered. As her soul prospers and her health increases, she will develop strength and a desire to prepare for the next assignment. (III John 1:2).

As she understands the role of Helper in the life of Adam, it is joyful, but a lot of work. It is so much work that it is impossible to do without the supernatural dispensation of Holy Spirit. That is why she must go slowly and allow the Lord to lead her and fend for her. The deception *thing* is very real in these situations. Satan determines what is needed to anesthetize her and reinforces it with glitter and trinkets that she likes. Remember, Satan studied Eve to know her. Under his anesthesia, he can rewire her values and her emotions and help her ignore or justify what is not right for her.

Be aware that a good-looking single woman of God can be a man magnet. Her inner beauty and presence have an appeal to men. I remember how men just wanted to be around me wherever I was. It often became embarrassing, and I became arrogant and somewhat annoyed by it. Thankfully, God sat me down and had me realize the attraction was the Light of Christ within me. He was overshadowing my looks with His presence. So, I started using this understanding as a tool to witness about what Christ means to me. I would say, "You are not as interested in me as you think, but that is okay. What is most appealing about me is something you can have without me. It is the Spirit of Christ, and you don't need me to have Him." It was amazing to see how well it worked. It was an interesting angle for reaching souls for Christ.

So, to clarify, Eve is a married human Helper. She is married to Adam or to Jesus. Her wisdom is beyond her human thinking and that of a basic Helper. Eve knows God. She knows God's Word and is lit with the wisdom and Love of God for her life. She hears the voice of the Good Shepherd (God) only. (John 10:14).

Women need to understand that being married to Christ is technically a more targeted dispensation of Love from Christ. He is

Savior to the entire Body of Christ, the Church. When Jesus agreed to be husband to all unassigned human Helpers, this was a big deal. Eve can leverage being married to The Holy. Eve knows her existence starts in the spirit realm for leadership. Not being assigned to an Adam, rocks! Also, know that Holy Spirit is always there to help His Helpers.

Some Helpers will spend much of their lives looking for a husband, and as a result, feel incomplete. Instead, see this as an opportunity to get all your kinks worked out with faithfulness, care, and discipline. What is your report card score for your existing marriage to Jesus? You must be fully prepared to be rightly assigned to an Adam. All sons of God who desire to have you will have to line up behind Jesus and make a request for you to the Father.

Sex Outside of Marriage (Fornication)

"God wants you to be holy and to stay away from sexual sins."
—I Thessalonians 4:3 New Century Version

Know that sex is a beautiful spiritual act gifted to a marriage and created by God. If misused, sex can be disgusting and deadly. Fornication is the name given by God for the abuse of His special gift. This type of sex builds emotional soul ties and addiction. It can invite other demonic attachments and could yield to the conception of a male's seed that is often unwanted and seen as inconvenient. It can create out-of-control emotions, including "the gotta have it" nature.

Sex outside of a covenant marriage relationship is animal and immoral. In the bedroom, you are alone physically, but in the spirit dimension, you have an audience, and God is typically not invited. You are never alone. It is animal, and your audience is not holy.

In marriage, sex is a good and perfect gift from the Lord, made by God. But regarding fornication, the Apostle Paul wrote in a letter to the Corinthian church (I Corinthians 6:18 NIV), "Flee from sexual immorality. All other sins a person commits are outside the body, but whoever sins sexually, sins against their own body."

He is saying sins are seeds planted *outside* of the body. However, sexual sins are seeds planted *within* the body. All sin has consequences. Yet, with sexual sin (against your own body), the seeds are buried within; there is damage done within, like self-implosions, impacting emotions, instilling fear, and exposing oneself to many other subtle but deadly situations.

Satan would like for us to value the natural or physical realm as most important in life. He tempts us to believe the physical is most important, including sets of symbols, systems, and measures for success with carefully crafted thoughts that lead away from authentic Christian living.

The Word of God makes it very clear about how to come to God. Jesus said, "…I am the way, the truth, and the life: no man cometh unto the Father, but by me." (John 14:6). Jesus cleans us up and makes us presentable. As we go, by faith, Jesus and Holy Spirit agree with our spirits in truth, and we are ready to spend time with the Father.

Fornication breaks your spirit. The Apostle Paul reminds us to "Keep yourselves from sexual promiscuity. Learn to appreciate and give dignity to your body, not abusing it, as is so common among those who know nothing of God." (I Thessalonians 4:1-4 MSG).

The enemy of God has been masterful in developing a culture that accepts all related behaviors leading to lust of the flesh, misguided attachments, fornication, and other actions that can become deadly habits (unforgiveness, anger, fear, and other unleashed emotions). A person who is prone to committing fornication is being entangled with thoughts and behaviors, imagined or real, that stand in the way of sanctification and right living before God.

So, why can't we just live together?

Under God, living this way places you outside of the protection of Father God. (John 4:17-24). It is dangerous for a Helper because you have attempted to attach yourself to an Adam who God did not assign to you. He is not your leader and has no spiritual alignment with Christ. In the court of heaven, you have no rights. You are an abomination to yourself, having been deceived by the enemy of God.

Little respect can be given to one who self-sabotages, but the grace from God, which is His Love, is always available.

You are beautiful and priceless. But living this way is out of order. Selling yourself short and making yourself feel good about it is the deceiver's plan. I know; I have been deceived, too — but not anymore.

Marriage looks like commitment to life... for life. You, as your Adam's Helper, must be willing to submit to his leadership because he loves you as Christ loves the Church. His love looks like respect and sacrifice for you (and your babies). You follow him as he follows Christ.

Is it possible that he is not the one?

A man who does not know God is not a son of God. In order to be a son of God, he must have been granted a new life in Christ. Otherwise, he is a son of man and does not know or respect the Father. He is a *son of man*.

Pray for the next steps. Go forth walking in Romans 12:2, which says, "And be not conformed to this world: but be ye transformed by the renewing of your mind, that ye may prove what is that good, and acceptable, and perfect, will of God."

See small but powerful prayers in Extra Help for Helpers (B) Prayer Scripts.

Eve Unmarried

Eve Restored

CHAPTER 7

Eve Unmarried

"...The unmarried woman or the virgin is concerned
about the matters of the Lord, how to be holy *and*
set apart both in body and in spirit..."
— I Corinthians 7:34 Amplified Bible

Ifyou are a believer, being unmarried in the natural means you are married to Christ in the spirit. Once in Christ, you are an Eve.

This is not a detour discussion about the Church. However, to understand the enormous territory of your Christ's work, you must consider the Church. Metaphorically, scripture (Revelations 19:7, Ephesians 5:27) refers to the Church as the Bride of Christ. Given the sections, regions, systems, organizations, and territories, the Church depicts an image that parallels the many workings of the human body. You cannot look at it in its traditional sense with denominational designations, like Methodist, Pentecostal, or Lutheran. Christ is the Head of the Church, and His Body is strong and varied.

For example, in scripture, a man named Lazarus had two sisters. Mary was not the type who would jump into hospitality-type activities like her sister, Martha. Instead, Mary focused on Jesus and His teaching. She pursued the gift of righteousness and the Love of God the Father. Her sister Martha had the gift of hospitality and comfort, so she poured her love out for Christ differently.

Every born-again believer is a unique member of the Body of Christ. We are not competitors. We have special gifts and talents that work nicely within the fellowship where we belong.

As a single woman, your goal is to seek God for the reason and purpose of your life. What dreams and visions have been placed within you that need more attention through prayer and meditation on God's Word?

Caring for Christ and His world is an exciting assignment to have. Christ is your Adam, Savior, High Priest, and elder brother. The leadership and related issues with Christ's work are far-reaching and impactful. There is a boatload of tasks to do, and many things that need prayer. Your purpose will become better defined as you grow in this. Knowing by faith, God, through His Word, makes it clear that He is working His plan for each of us in a way only He could do. He said that His thoughts are not our thoughts. He knows the plan. Christ charts the way and brings order, all with the free gifts and benefits that come with being God's child. No worries, it includes the protection, health, joy, peace, wisdom and understanding, freedom from fear, light burdens, and easy yokes or partnerships. (*See* Helper Benefit Package for additional Helper benefits.)

Being married to Christ is the perfect training ground to be prepared and polished for the next assignment. You get to learn and use the three facets of love, as inspired by Matthew 22:37-40:

1. You will become orderly and organized. (I Corinthians 14:40).
2. You will shape your core values, and dump every trace of wrong in your life, embracing only the good. (Psalms 1:3, 19:14).
3. As your soul gets fit, your physical health, strength, and countenance are restored. (III John 1:2).

We know that Helper power is unstoppable through Christ. A Helper does not need to be an Adam; she only needs to be Eve, who is a Helper with the wisdom of God.

Main Point:

A Helper does not need to be an Adam; she only needs to be Eve, who is a Helper with the wisdom of God.

Eve Restored

What is important to remember is that Christ's birth, death, and resurrection restored God's intentions for us. The Office of Adam and The Office of Eve were restored. Jesus assumed our sin and bad decisions. Meanwhile, Satan established sinful strongholds in the world (culture) that cause the plan of redemption to be essential to our survival. Jesus brings us Light. He is The Way, the Truth, and The Life to all who will receive Him. This redemption plan is the only way back to God the Father.

Main Point:

Christ's birth, death, and resurrection restored God's intentions for us.

CHAPTER 8

Adam, Son of God

- Introduction to Adam
- The Nature of Adam
- Words of Wisdom About Adam
- Adam's Understanding of the Supernatural Gift of Eve
- Exercises God-given Dominion over His Life
- Misaligned Adam
- Adam, the Father of Sons
- Adam, the Father of Daughters
- Adam, as Stepdad

Adam, Son of God

Introduction to Adam

> "Jesus answered them,
> 'Is it not written in your law, I said, Ye are gods'"? —John 10:34

He is a king, a son of God. Jesus is Adam's Lord, Savior, and elder brother. Jesus is the King over all kings, but Adam is a king and has full dominion over his household and the earth. Adam has a physical body but, on the inside, he is not all human. By faith, he has the mind of Christ, and his body is the temple of Holy Spirit. The Word of God flows richly into his bloodstream. He is redeemed, righteous, and made free from sin, and now, a son of God.

If we look at Old Testament accounts of men who stood and lived in the presence of God (Adam, Abraham, Noah, King Ahasuerus (Xerxes), David, Joseph, and others), they stood, covering their households. A king's household must be in order. Marriage is an assignment by God, for the son and daughter of God. Rebekah was born to help Isaac; God had it all planned. Of course, Abraham was "all up in" the vision with Holy Spirit, who gave him specific instructions about where to go and what pedigree was required for Isaac. (Genesis 24:45).

If you just go and pick a mate *because* — or for any other reason than for a God-given marriage, I do not recommend it. Stand on your holy ground and send him away, using the full assistance of Holy Spirit. God can remove him without any lasting impact to your emotions.

Main Point:

Marriage is an assignment, by God, for the son and daughter of God.

The Nature of Adam

Adam, according to Genesis 1:26, represents the anointing in the position assigned by God to have dominion and serve in headship over the earth. He is the leader of his household, the Helper (woman), children, other younger relatives, and employees. His birth name will be John, Jerry, or Michael, for example, but in Christ, he is designated *Adam*, who represents a male containing the seed and anointing of his lineage as the son of God.

God created man in the image of God the Holy Trinity — a human speaking Spirit, walking out the image of God in the earth. He is prayerfully creative and loves all that he is and is to become. He is spiritually, mentally, and physically strong. God gave man power to have rule or dominion over the whole earth. He was told by God to "...Be fruitful, and multiply, and replenish the earth, and subdue it: and have dominion over the fish of the sea, and over the fowl of the air, and over every living thing that moveth upon the earth." (Genesis 1:28)

In the earthly realm, Adam is the leader. He is the overseer of his household. He trains his children (seed), and he is the provider. He protects and secures his household. He is strong, patient, and kind. He brings holiness and works with Eve to bring peace. He has dreams and visions from God, special gifts, and the ability to plan, communicate, and provide. He accepts Eve as a gift from God and with the obedience and Blood-covered protection of our Lord; he receives Eve. She is a good and perfect gift from the Lord. She is customized (looks, personality, faith, and anointing) for Adam. Adam is a man of God, a man of honor, and a son of God. Eve is a daughter of God and a woman of wisdom.

The brother is good! He is among gods of the earth. (Psalm 82:6). His presence and countenance are something to behold. He would have to be if he is a child of the highest God! He sees (real time, through vision or dream) and speaks, making declarations and decrees, just like God. He is a king, the younger brother of Jesus. If he embraces his position, he is to be honored.

Main Point:

Adam represents a male containing the seed and anointing of his lineage as the son of God.

Words of Wisdom About Adam

Sons of God are royalty. They must be strong, responsible, and of good character. The Book of Proverbs is the book of wisdom and outlines the characteristics of wise people. It also tells how to avoid evil, traps, and fools. In Chapter 31, the message from King Lemuel's mother addresses two areas for kings to avoid and exercise self-control: strange women and drinking, which both lead to intoxication. She also addresses the impact of alcohol use on the brain and memory, saying it erases critical landmarks that destroy families.

She starts this passage by establishing her position and right as a mother and because she gave birth to him; she has maintained that spiritual connection and an understanding of his vulnerabilities. The Bible has recorded few instances where women (Helpers) are giving direct instruction to a man.

This prophetess-Helper-mother is best qualified to give these words to her son, Lemuel, but understands that it is a rare opportunity. With wisdom, she is aware of how her family lineage could be negatively impacted if her son got involved with ungodly Helpers, so she lightly addresses it. Then, in verses 10 through 31 describes for him the traits of a good woman and how he benefits from having her as a wife. She wants her Helper nature to be connected to Holy Spirit and her son's soon-to-be assigned Helper (wife). This is his "rite of passage" to the good life.

Main Point:

A man does not respond to Helper teachers. Holy Spirit will manage the communications as Eve prays.

Adam's Understanding of the Supernatural Gift of Eve

"So ought men to love their wives as their own bodies.
He that loveth his wife loveth himself." —Ephesians 5:28

Adam sees her as a gift from God. He understands Eve's office and lets her operate therein. He is no match for her, and she is no match for him. She has access to God when she needs help with things for Adam. She can see things, pray, and be available to help. It is a divine office —Eve as Helper. She is chief confidante to Adam. They have become one, spiritually. Her prayers are his prayers; his prayers are her prayers. (I Corinthians 7:14). She can ask the Father to give him a deeper understanding of an issue he does not see clearly, which brings help without her having to teach.

This relationship is in the Name of Jesus, our High Priest, in the order of Melchizedek. Her office is ordained and highly ordered. This is big in the spirit realm. How can two become one? Two equals one? It is a supernatural designation — a unit within God's Kingdom. So, to fuss or cause hurt (physically or emotionally) means you are hurting yourself.

Main Point:

The *oneness* in marriage is a supernatural designation (1+1=1).

Exercises God-given Dominion over His Life

Acting as Adam, his life history proves that he is who he says he is. The following characteristics or questions will be evident if an Eve is to consider his leadership in her life. This is not a complete list of everything your Adam must possess or be. It is meant to help you see these good qualities in other people as you live and grow. You can collect these qualities for your own prayer request for your Adam assignment.

10 Essentials that must be in place. No tradeoffs:

1. He knows he is a son of God.
2. He loves and is fearless.
3. He must have a prospering soul.

4. He must have a personal testimony of the Gospel of Jesus Christ.
5. He must be a student of the Bible.
6. He prays and meditates on the Word of God.
7. He has strong faith.
8. He has discipline and a good work ethic.
9. He makes good use of time.
10. He has health and strength.

Qualities to establish a great Adam.

This is a time for you to be in fellowship with Holy Spirit. Your meetings with Holy Spirit can be very detailed. This is because God knows all there is to know about Adam and you. God also has big plans for each of you to bring Him great glory.

Questions to ask about your Adam.

1. Can I follow his leadership (good times, stress, and disappointment)?
   a. How does he make decisions?
   b. Does he have an obvious prayer life?
   c. Can you see his values?
   d. Is he trustworthy?
2. Does he do what he says he will do when he says he will do it?
3. Where is his faith?
4. Does he have a prayer partner?
5. Is he a son of God?
6. What are his values?
7. Is he consistent over time?
8. What is his relationship with the women in his family?
9. How does he handle his finances and business (if any)?

10. Does he have a vision for his life?

11. Does he care for himself?

12. Do his words and thoughts speak life?

13. Does he have a spiritual covering large enough for my mind, body (temple), and faith?

14. Has he ever been married? What happened?

15. Does he respect my father or guardian?

16. Does he have a prospering soul? (III John 1:2).

As in scripture, God will reach to any point in the world to get an Eve for His son of God, Adam. For example, in scripture, as with Isaac and Rebekah, they needed to flow in obedience and with the blessing of God. Abraham sent his servant back to his home country to get a young virgin for his son, Isaac; it was Rebekah. (Genesis 24).

A challenge for a Helper is to not get in front of the process. Being that she is a Helper, she can quickly jump into the Helper mode and *rope* an Adam in. With the proper match, Adam competes with Eve to do more loving things for her than she does for him. "They have it going on."

Main Points:

- Do not step out in front of God to *rope* Adam in.
- God needs you to be quick to listen, slow to speak, and slow to anger.

Misaligned Adam

A misaligned Adam is, by nature, evil, and he is not of God. He is a son of man, not a son of God. Do not even consider him as a candidate for marriage. He is physically stronger, and if he does not know and love Jesus as his Savior and elder brother, he is not ready for help, and you are in danger. You cannot fix this, so please do not try. Turn that (and all issues related to him) over to God and move away. Many women think they can fix this. Know that he is not ready for you now and may never be ready (God's plan).

It is challenging for a Helper (Eve) if her Adam does not fully understand her Helper nature. He needs to, by faith, receive her as a dispensation of the Holy Spirit of God just for him. He cannot receive this without faith.

Men are always in warfare. He may not be aware of the spiritual origin of his battles. However, he does not expect help in war. The world culture has trained him to operate without help. So, Eve will have to go easy with all that she has within her to help him. Soon, like King David in scripture, he will see that his help "cometh from the Lord" and much of that help is already within his household — Eve. (Psalm 121:2).

Soon, he must realize that you (as Eve) live to help him in his life with God. He will come to know that in the *oneness* of marriage, God honors him. God honors and loves him enough to do it Adam's way. You help him as he journeys with God, his faith grows, and the miraculous takes place.

Know that prior to marriage, God considers if He can honor Adam by going through him to love you. God wants to be sure you understand and honor Adam, so the oneness process runs smoothly. Adam must have a Christlike nature, so his love for you is like Christ's Love for the Church. We know how much Christ loves His Church.

God → Christ → Eve   or   God → Adam → Eve

Scripture admonishes us to know that "Every good gift and every perfect gift is from above, and cometh down from the Father of lights, with whom is no variableness, neither shadow of turning." (James 1:17). There are no almost-perfect gifts or soon-to-be-perfect gifts from God. God only gives perfect gifts. God gives Eve perfect leadership.

> **Main Point:**
>
> God considers if He can honor Adam by going through him to love you.

Adam, the Father of Sons

A dad must show godly strength and restraint to his son. He must raise him to appreciate and honor his mother and have a strong regard for his siblings. Through Dad, he grows to know his strength and total self-control. He must learn of the power in the spirit realm. He should know the Holy Trinity and the benefit of living in the Kingdom of God as Adam.

A boy must be taught to see all family females as Helpers, a gift from God to help keep things running smoothly. Helpers solve problems and are dependable members of the family.

Adam, the Father of Daughters

Adam with Young Daughters.

All girls are *daddy's girls*. Daddy is her leader and protector. The gentle treatment, together with discipline given by her leader, is required. It must be understood that a dad mirrors the covering upon his daughter so that her expectations for love and safety are set and reinforced. She belongs to her father, Adam. Her developmental stages are safe when her daddy is guided by God the Father, with an Eve by his side. Provision is met. Godliness is expected. Baby girl is trained to respect her father, Adam.

Earlier on, she has certain powerful qualities that include:

- fertility for a nation of people placed in her ovaries at birth.
- words that are fruitful gifts but can cut.
- the gift of influence.
- creativity that is connected to the fruitfulness given to her at birth.

Girls have power from the start of life. Scientifically speaking, every little infant girl has two small sacks called ovaries that contain millions of unfertilized eggs. She is the keeper of that many potential people. A major assignment to be given to a Helper from the start.

The enemy of God attempts to kill and destroy her, using the justice system, crushing self-esteem and self-worth, or using abuse and self-hate.

Puberty for a little Helper is a time when she must be closely watched by her mother and father. The responsibility of these blessed parents is to recognize the *newness* of life for her, which becomes obvious to all and to protect her and *suffer* with her through this training period, which is called *puberty*. She is vulnerable at this age (physically, mentally, and spiritually). The words and prayers of parents serve as healing balms to balance the possible roller coaster of experiences.

Daughters should not be compared to sons. All her life she has *princess* written all over her and in many environments, she can be encouraged and influenced to not be Eve-like, but to be as an Adam.

Her dad's love and nurturing raises the bar for her future Adam, and she has no reason to compromise. She *is* a princess.

Main Point:

Her developmental stages are safe when her daddy is guided by God the Father, with an Eve by his side.

Adam with Older Daughters.

A dad is his daughter's first exposure to male leadership. He demonstrates the guidance, protection, and care that is expected. If a guy treats your daughter like "one of the guys," then his motive is suspect, and she does not have to settle. It is simply because she knows good treatment by what she has seen in her dad and brothers.

Adam, as Stepdad.

Believe that God the Father considered these precious children when He considered this assignment for Eve. God's Love must come through your Adam to raise them. They become the olive plants around his table, Mom (Helper, hopefully an Eve) being the fruitful vine growing around his house. (Psalm 128:3). A child being referred to as an olive plant in scripture denotes beauty, strength, and of a good heritage.

Becoming the father of a nonbiological son is also a work from God the Father for an Adam. Healing will be needed in many areas as the child has been living life for a period without the leadership of a father. A stepdad will need to identify areas of pain, emotional lack, and anger, all with love. This love is a spirit-engrafted love customized by God for this son and his new dad.

Becoming the father of a nonbiological daughter is a work from God the Father for an Adam. If her mother has received the *okay* from God to marry this Adam, then all is set. This father and daughter relationship is not instant, but will be built over time through consistency, sacrifice, and trust. Do not allow the deceiver to claim this gift (the daughter).

Holy Spirit must help with every dimension of these new relationships.

CHAPTER 9

The Marriage of Adam and Eve

- Prepping for Marriage
- The Institution of Marriage
- Helpers from the Eyes of God for You
- Miracle in the Oneness
- The Marriage Bed
- Helpers Without Wisdom (HWW)
- The Sacredness of a Helper's Household
- Church Life for Adam and Eve

CHAPTER 9

The Marriage of Adam and Eve

Woman was specially created by God. She was given all the attributes needed to be a Helper. Her role as a godly wife is priceless. In her godly role, she finds fulfillment, passion, and excitement. She is rewarded by God for staying in her appointed place. Her prayer life includes a prayer component ordained by God for the assigned Adam and his sphere.

Prepping for Marriage

Before I was married, I was Eve married to Christ. However, I began to desire a life with an Adam. Never ignore your desires. If they are not desires within your heart from God, they are likely to be lusts, which are sins placed there by the deceiver. God said in His Word that He will give you the desires of your heart. Pray these scriptures: Psalm 37:4 and Psalm 20:4. Afterward, go to Extra Help for Helpers (B) Prayer Scripts.

There were some specific points that Holy Spirit had me pray and meditate on. These prayer points really helped align me to receive my Adam before I was even aware of the plan or his name. One point was that I knew I was going to do great things. Therefore, my mate must have an umbrella that is bigger than mine, so I can fit my world within his comfortably. Speaking of comfort, the next point was that I needed to be as comfortable with him in the room as if it were just me and Jesus there. And finally, not having a name, I prayed that he and I were both going through the set of life experiences that would work perfectly in us for God's glory.

It is a pleasure to report that these three points became very fruitful. With this answered prayer, everything continues to be used for us and for God's glory.

Being married to Christ is also an office. Jesus knows. You are literally attached to Him in the spirit. So much so that when the time comes for you to marry (be assigned to an Adam), you will need to get God's permission to change offices. God is a jealous God, and He will not be happy about just anyone walking into your life. Holy Spirit will prepare you and your Adam. It is not your job to hunt, pick, capture, and marry someone. Marriage for a Helper is an assignment. It is a team effort with joy.

Main Point:

God is a jealous God, and He will not be happy about just anyone walking into your life.

The Institution of Marriage

God is so into His creation of the institution called *marriage* that He made a consideration for Adam. Eve considers Adam before God and God considers Adam with Eve before Himself, like Christ to the Church. Her faithfulness to Adam is honoring God, who makes that union work.

This marriage must receive approval from God the Father. Instead of God looking at you directly, He is looking at the marriage, the oneness of it, and sees the two as one. How can 1+1=1? (*See* Genesis 2:24). This is not human math. It is a supernatural spiritual disposition that joins two human spirits. The two agree (with God) to go in the same direction with Adam as the leader.

Here are a few thoughts I have experienced through prayer and revelation:

- Marriage is a supernatural occurrence.
- God makes two people one in the Spirit.
- God respects Adam and will help you honor him. You may not agree with his way all the time. Go to God for help.
- God will help. God will bless Adam's way if you honor it.
- God will bless Adam's household if you stake your ground as Helper in his life.

Main Points:

- The *oneness* of *marriage* is a supernatural spiritual disposition that joins two human spirits.
- Make sure that you *do marriage* God's way. Otherwise, it could be deadly, dangerous, or downright miserable. But do not give up. Your path will become clearer as you move toward salvation.

Miracle in the Oneness

It is challenging for a Helper when her Adam does not fully understand the Helper's nature. This understanding cannot be received without faith.

If you feel like you need to scream, fuss, and speak the next step, that is what your Helper friend (not girlfriend) is here for. You can tell Holy Spirit (your Helper), as a way of releasing the emotional buildup around an issue. The conversation with Him is translated into a prayer. A Helper's petitions for her Adam are always heard.

This Helper assignment is not always a walk in the park, because the old nature (the "neck-moving" person) wants to be expressed. I had never been this way before! When I arrived at the "slow to speak" point, I did not know what to say. Everything I thought of saying did not bring honor, had a selfish motive, and did not advance the cause. So, I remained speechless and prayerful until I saw the next step.

If you know what you need to have happen, then speak the Word of God over the situation. But just before you do, ask Holy Spirit if your thought is as clear as it seems. Is there something else that is not lining up first?

Main Point:

A Helper's petitions for her Adam are always heard.

As Helper, I get to see my household vision through my *Helper* eyes, not as a wife with her own interests. This is the only way to honor Adam. A wife can love her Adam, but she can only honor him out of her Eve office.

Why is it okay to not look out for myself? Consider this, by faith:

- Love and honor are transferred from God the Father to Jesus,
- Love and honor are transferred from God the Father to Adam,
- I can honor them (Jesus and Adam) because their love for me is authentic and customized by God, who loves me. So, I am covered. I am loved.

Before marriage, God considers if He can honor Adam, and go through him to love you. God wants to be sure you understand and honor Adam, so the oneness that He gives runs smoothly.

If God cannot see this for you in that marriage, He will say "no." If God says "no," accept it. Be emotional, like King David, in front of your loving Father, and ask Him to show you the path to correct (remove) that situation.

When Eve understands her position, Adam's struggles go away. The righteous prayers of Eve are bonds that firmly connect them to Christ.

With this union, you can see with the lens of your spouse. You do not see the difference as a point of contention, but as something to understand, within a dimension that you would not naturally see or know. You can express your true feelings, which will surprisingly line up with the resolution planned by the Father.

Her husband praises her:

> "Many women do noble things, but you surpass
> them all." —Proverbs 31:29 NIV

Main Points:

- Oneness in marriage is a miracle and will mature overtime, with Holy Spirit's help.
- This Helper assignment is not always a walk in the park.
- God supernaturally develops the oneness within your marriage as His children.

The Marriage Bed

There is nothing in the human experience like the sexual expression of Adam to his Eve and Eve to her leader. It is sacred and can bring about rage when it is threatened or violated. Know that God designed and created this loving, giving, planting, and release for this special couple whom He holds in high regard. Adam literally yields his strength to her. (Proverbs 31:3).

It is critical that any prior sexual encounters (thought, deed, expectation, envisioned, or imagined) outside of marriage be confessed as sin, uprooted from your heart, with a renewed mind, in Jesus' Name. (Matthew 15:13).

This is a healing experience. There is no performance. All prior experience, methods, procedures, and selfish expectations are a thing of the past. All the stress, criticism, and anxiety are no longer issues. This is so critical that children of God do not bring prior sexual relation experience to this ordained healing experience. Because you come in spirit and truth, Satan is not allowed. It's just the two of you! When you have this for the rest of your life, responsible to one person to enjoy, under God, with God, it all becomes new and good. It's like pushing the reset button and allowing the love you are in to take over. The reason it must be new is that ground zero for this experience starts with that spiritual oneness, which is: 1+1=1 or Adam + Eve = *One*.

This is a supernatural designation that strips away all the vain things imagined and builds you up in your most holy faith. You can partake of Holy Communion (remember Christ) and pray in the spirit on the way to a sexual expression as one. No shame, you two are in the presence of God.

The bed is special. It is a significant part of the oneness God spoke about marriage. Couples in Christ can use Holy Spirit and their prospering souls to enhance the experience, making it a customized, healing experience. Your heavenly Father knows what you stand in need of. Your soil is ripe to receive seed, and he has been prepared to plant seed (spiritually and physically). Sex is also a spiritual encounter, which is why it must be between married couples (with the oneness). It is an agreement with God to receive this gift of extreme beauty and intimacy. Marriage is the license of the Kingdom to enter therein. So, it is not really *sexing* as the world defines it. It is an intercourse of Love. Knowing that your heavenly Father's alias is *Love,* where will His Love take you every time? "… for God is love." (1 John 4:8).

Couples in Christ cannot use the world's ways to shape their relationship. God will use your imagination for this experience.

Eve cannot withhold or make him pay to be with her. And Adam cannot be locked into the world's value system and expectations on this topic. It must be based on Love from God, given to you to express to each other. In scripture, Adam's love for Eve is expressed as Christ's Love for the Church. It is unconditional. He brings that Love. She brings Love also, but more important than that, Love is the dispensation that allows her to honor him. Adam needs to be honored and appreciated more than loved. Momma can love him, but Eve must honor him. (Ephesians 5:25, Colossians 3:18, Ephesians 5:28).

Main Point:

It is critical that children of God do not bring prior sexual relation experience to this ordained healing experience. Sex was created by God and gifted to His children.

Helper Without Wisdom (HWW)

A Helper who is detached from God is windblown with her skills working against God and the work she has been assigned. She operates as an HWW. Someone once said when the woman of the household is not happy, no one else is happy. Satan has deceived her to think that she should be an Adam, not an Eve. She can keep the peace and go through the motions, but is she that vine circling the household? Are her children the olive plants round about her table, according to Psalm 128:3?

Helpers who are detached from Christ are often control seekers. They appear smart and can outsmart Adam in front of the children and others. With this control, they feel a false sense of peace when they have the dominating voice over things. She is a Helper when it is convenient, but is not walking in God's will for her life. She is unable to help the people to whom she has been assigned. She cannot help them reach their God-given potential in life because she lacks the godly wisdom of Eve.

An HWW, in Christ, may simply not understand her placement and is in a deceived state. She is dangerous, having the potential assignments from God but living outside of the Kingdom of God. She is a danger to her Adam, because she may still have a selfish nature, being unaware of her office. Therefore, she can be tricked again and again. Even though she is a child of God, she continues to help Satan, because it is in her nature to help. This Helper, if not married, must not use her own foolish thoughts and shiny objects to select an Adam.

Main Points:

- A Helper who is independent of Christ is an HWW.
- An HWW is windblown with her skills working against God. She cannot win, even though her life seems good.

Biblical Examples of Helpers Without Wisdom

There are some powerful stories of women in scripture who were Helpers not fully able to help God. Their unbelief and lack of wisdom rendered them foolish, many times causing them to overhelp or under help. Definitely Helpers, *yes*, but without the wisdom to see the deceiver in their situations. We know, through the power of Christ, prayer for wisdom and understanding are essential. (James 1:5).

Biblical Examples of Helpers Without Wisdom:

Eve Genesis 3:2	Had a conversation with Satan and succumbed to his deception. Dialogues with Satan never work for human Helpers. **Divine judgment**: Put Adam in place to protect her.
Delilah Judges 16:4-31	The Philistine woman who was paid to discover Samson's strength. **Divine judgment**: No word was given. Many were killed within the building that collapsed when pulled down by Samson. She may have been there also.
Queen Jezebel I Kings 16:31 II Kings 9:7-10	A Phoenician princess, married Ahab, King of Israel. She killed the prophets of Jehovah to remain in power. Established idolatry in Israel. **Divine judgment**: Was devoured and eaten by dogs.
Job's wife Job 2:9-10	Told Job to curse God and die. **Divine judgment**: No word was given. She was already in great pain, distress, and on course for self-destruction.
Herodias Matthew 14:3-12	Deserted her first husband, Herod Philip, and married Antipas (his half-brother). Antipas divorced his first wife to marry Herodias. These actions were sins condemned by John the Baptist. She used her Helper daughter to have John the Baptist beheaded. **Divine judgment**: No word was given; however, evil behaviors can lead to death.
Michal II Samuel 6:16	Daughter of Saul, given to David to marry. Tried to shame King David for dancing in praise to God. **Divine judgment**: Closed her womb. No children ever.
Vashti Esther 1:9-2:17	Queen of Ahasuerus (Xerxes), the King of Persia. She refused to help the King when he requested. **Divine judgment**: Received a divorce and could never be in the King's presence.
Lot's wife Genesis 19:26	Told to go and not look back. She looked back. **Divine judgment**: Turned into a pillar of salt.
Miriam Num 12:10-15	Moses' sister bad-mouthed him for marrying outside his race, claiming that Moses was not the only prophet among them. **Divine judgment**: Was stricken with leprosy and put outside of the camp until the leprosy disappeared (seven days, in answer to Moses' prayer for her).

Jesus used a parable in scripture about ten virgins who were awaiting the bridegroom. The bridegroom is Christ. Five virgins were wise; five virgins were unwise. The wise virgins had their lamps trimmed and burning with additional oil to keep them burning. The unwise virgins could not meet the bridegroom because they were not prepared. When the call came, they had to go to buy oil for their lamps. When they returned, the door was shut, and the bridegroom refused to let them in. (Matthew 25:1). The wise Helper is expecting Christ and always working to glorify Him.

Main Point:

An Eve must operate with an angel posted at the door of her mouth. (Psalm 141:3).

The Sacredness of a Helper's Household

Clarification of a Helper's household is needed. This ownership is not ruling Adam's territory or his domain. It is the spiritual circle drawn around his territory, including family, networks, and relationships. This is a Helper's watch. She speaks God's Word to have angels encamp round about it (Psalm 34:7) and she reminds God that Jesus asked that He keep them from evil. (John 17:15).

Your household is Jesus' territory, and you are on watch. It is so important that Helpers understand this. On this prayer watch, invite Holy Spirit to sit with you and show you all the things you cannot do anything about, areas of protection needed, and a lighted way for Adam's work and relationships. As part of the Helper's watch, Eve must encircle Adam's territory by identifying the elders, the children, the disabled, the orphan, and the poor. Where is love needed (including salvation)? Determine what acts of kindness you can show and what would lighten their burdens. Envision your prayer life, including praying scripture over your household. Like Psalm 91 and Proverbs 14:1, or the prayer of Jabez for your Adam, as stated in I Chronicles 4:9-10. How about

"Thy kingdom come, thy will be done," or "Deliver us from evil," as in Matthew 6:13? God's Word is the secret sauce to your environment; it is powerful. Even if there is no Adam, your household is Jesus' territory, and you are on watch.

In Jesus' Name, you can take authority over land and weather conditions, forbidding all evil intentions. You can ask Holy Spirit to block ungodly dreams and things that trespass against your children. Using a scripture, create your own family benediction that you say over the coming and going of your family. My favorite benediction is "The Lord bless and keep you from evil." Every Word of God is blessed, so you can pray any part of it.

Ask Holy Spirit (the Holy Helper) to assist you in keeping all things done in decency and order. (I Corinthians 14:40).

If you are a mother raising children with no Adam, see your marriage to Jesus in the spirit realm, giving Him authority over your home, children, and all you have. You may need your Jesus to help make your household a sacred environment.

Eve's environment

- What is a sacred space? Heaven, Kingdom living.
- Household strategy for sacred spaces:
  - sacred space where the Word of God can be studied.
  - sacred chambers include the kitchen, living room, bedroom, and bathroom.
- Once a week, do a *stuff-control* exercise:
  - Everything has an address.
  - Save or keep?
  - Is this working for us?
  - Decency and in order.

Main Point:

A Helper's household is the spiritual circle drawn around Adam's territory, including family, networks, and relationships.

Church Life for Adam and Eve

While this idea of Adam and Eve in the Church is vast, it is much more simplified as we have our households established under God. We now know what God says about who we are to Him and what we are here to do, which is to show forth His love and glory.

As we all come into the full understanding of God's will, we pray for the execution of the Word of God toward the people of God as we grow into perfect alignment.

Eve knows that at church, like at home, Adam and Father God are her protectors. Holy Spirit is right there to coach their behaviors according to the Word and will of God. Ministry and causes should both edify and provide ways to serve.

CHAPTER 10

The Prayer Life of Eve

"Prayer leaps over all barriers, stops at no distances and balks at no obstacles because it is in touch with the infinite resources of heaven."
—Dr. M.R. DeHaan

- What is the Prayer Life of Eve?
- Prayer Framework
- Worship
- Gratitude
- Daily Petitions
- Daily Renewal
- Daily Defense
- Journal
- Sleep
- Prayer Partnering

The Prayer Life of Eve

Prayer and the voice (Word) of God are what make Eve most valuable. Adam can put his entire household upon this woman of God, the appointed one. Imagine living life with a piece of the light of God in human form. So, after thanksgiving and praise, her top priority is for her Adam and his dominion. From kids to employees and their spheres, then self-preservation.

She sees prayer as a 24/7 connection to God. It is life within the Kingdom. The atmosphere within the Kingdom is love, illuminated by the power of God. Our prayer keeps us plugged in, strengthened, and positioned in the presence of God. Life in the Kingdom is the realm in which we live, move, and have our being. (Acts 17:28). We need a prayer framework. This framework is a way of thinking about your relationship with God and remaining connected to Him. Intelligent prayer is how we are spiritually nourished. In using this framework, Holy Spirit, along with our mind, body, and spirit must be involved. Scripture admonishes us to bless the Lord with our soul and all that is within us. When we pray, our body, thoughts, imagination, subconscious, and emotions are engaged.

What is the Prayer Life of Eve?

A connection to Holy Spirit is a natural part of the spirit of Eve. She has received her appointment and sees her value. She knows that without a constant prayer connection, her work and her role will not be as fruitful or build the best legacy for her family. She is a prayer warrior and, as a result, can do the impossible every day by faith in the Lord Jesus. An Eve who is detached from God is deadly and as powerful as a fallen angel with skills working against God and Adam.

Should she have a planned approach to daily prayer? Yes. You can build your prayer framework as you grow in this day by day. What follows is a good sample for spending time and staying connected to God daily.

Prayer Framework

Worship

Worshipping God is our best effort to hold Him in high regard above all others. We acknowledge His deity, greatness, power, and love in our lives. Worship is the connection we make through the spirit and truth to give glory to God the Father and the Lord Jesus Christ. To worship God, we must have chosen and received a new relationship with God, through Jesus, the Christ. This relationship lets us have a renewed mind centered on God and a heart that has no unconfessed sin. (See Romans 8:10, John 3:16).

Gratitude

A grateful heart fortifies our mind, body, and spirit. Thankfulness is the partner to worship. With gratitude, we acknowledge what God has done, what He is doing, and what we know He will do based on His Word and all the promises He has made to His children. We are thankful for all His provisions and for the opportunity to acknowledge His goodness and mercy toward us. We are grateful that He is dependable, faithful, and committed to a relationship with us. Each of us can lift those unique areas in our lives where God has blessed, protected, and helped us. We are full of so many answered prayers. The Apostle Paul reminds us in his letter to the Philippians, "Do not be anxious about anything, but in every situation, by prayer and petition, with thanksgiving, present your request to God." (Philippians 4:6 NIV). We are grateful that God's Love never ever fails.

Daily Petitions

Eve understands that to work without hardship, she needs the help of Holy Spirit. She also understands that her heavenly Father majors in the impossible. Make a list of everything on your mind. Use paper or create a list using your handheld device if you can do it without being distracted. She takes each thing (large or small) to God.

Daily Renewal

"...who healeth all thy diseases;" —Psalm 103:3

It is difficult to heal when we are busy, but God is willing and able. To be renewed and refreshed every day, spend fifteen to thirty minutes in prayer, scripture meditation, breathing, and stretching. Jesus said,

"Are you tired? Worn out? Burned out on religion? Come to me. Get away with me and you'll recover your life. I'll show you how to take a real rest. Walk with me and work with me—watch how I do it. Learn the unforced rhythms of grace. I won't lay anything heavy or ill-fitting on you. Keep company with me and you'll learn to live freely and lightly." (Matthew 11:28-30 MSG).

The joy of the Lord brings strength.

Daily Defense

For women who are in the Kingdom of God, we bear all the rights and privileges of being called His daughters, being able to call Him *Father*, our only Healer. We can go to Him, and He will give us His full attention!

"And will be a Father unto you, and ye shall be my sons and daughters, saith the Lord Almighty." —II Corinthians 6:18

Just for a few moments each day in prayer, use your imagination (putting it under the authority of Holy Spirit) to lay your body before God and ask Him to reset it. Speak to every cell in your body, every organ, every thought, instructing them to yield to the Father. Then ask the Father to cleanse each of them, sweeping away the waste wherever it may be and allowing it to exit your body appropriately and in order. Release anger, stress, fear, and unforgiveness that may be inside you. Allow God to do a sweep of your emotions, thoughts, and imagination. Remember the work and the investment God has made in you and assure Him that you desire to complete your assignment. Receive complete wholeness delivered by Christ. See in your mind the peace of God pouring into every cell, filling every organ, fully saturating your entire body like water into a sponge. And the peace of God, which surpasses every thought, will guard your hearts and your minds in Christ Jesus. Seal it with your faith and a grateful heart. Amen.

Journal

Eve must keep track. Her relationship with God is no exception. A journal is a book, normally bound and blank, used exclusively for your time and study with the Father. Like prayer, journaling helps free the mind, giving you more capacity to handle other things. We journal to keep our prayer life organized and effective, as instructed in I Timothy 2. We are told to make our request known, pray for others, and offer up prayers of thanksgiving. In our journal, we should designate a section for each of these categories according to I Timothy 2:1-4.

1. Prayers of Thanksgiving
2. Answered Prayers
3. Prayer Requests
4. Word of the Day
5. Prayers for Others
6. The Work – Your Assignments

Include in answered prayers, miracles, and one brief testimony (one or two statements). We see Holy Spirit handling our petitions for our household constantly. These are praise reports.

Sleep

Eve's sleep is sweet as God promised and is a prayer posture where reconcilement (in every dimension), healing, and spiritual gifts are given. Sleep is that supernatural activity assured and maintained by the proper spiritual environment. This is so special that God calls it "sweet sleep," which is a promise. "When thou liest down, thou shalt not be afraid: yea, thou shalt lie down, and thy sleep shall be sweet." (Proverbs 3:24).

Prayer Partnering

Eve understands the power of circled prayer, which includes the two or three gathered with another wise woman. By faith, bring a praise report, petitions, and the impossibilities (on your watch) for supernatural attention to the throne. Once each week works (15-60 minutes). Do not be late. The Father is always on time for prayer appointments.

It is important that we connect to the God force in our lives several times a day. With this habit, our future has just been sealed for a path beyond what we can imagine or think. We do not have the capacity to see the total picture of our lives, but staying connected to God is essential, for He said He knows the plans He has for us. (Jeremiah 29:11). God can make the impossible possible.

"Delight thyself also in the Lord;
and he shall give thee the desires of thine heart." —Psalm 37:4

CHAPTER 11

Recap of The Office

CHAPTER 11

※

Recap of The Office

All females are, by nature, God-designed Helpers.

This Office of Eve is counter cultural in our world today. We need to remember that the warfare has not changed. Satan is still much attracted to Eve and her assignments. He uses the position of Eve, whether she is a wife, mother, sister, or friend, to reinforce that Adam is not who he should be and that his difference must be controlled. Eve is multifaceted and a quick study. In her dysfunction, she knows (figures out) how to bring Adam down, be it Samson or Solomon.

In society, men tend to huddle. If they dishonor God by refusing His Son, Jesus, they cannot see Helpers for their value, but rather as a utility. A man can use brute force and psychological abuse to wrongfully manipulate his Eve, which is not the intent God has for him as her leader.

In the home, a Helper Without Wisdom often rules, but is out of order. As a result, she typically ends up single, or a single parent. The enemy of God has built his own unholy infrastructure in which we are tempted to operate.

The community of Helpers around the globe is always there to help, especially with the children.

The spiritual experience of the marriage bed has been replaced with pornography, fornication, adulterous activities, and ungodliness. The deceiver, the prince of the power of the air, uses the beauty and fashion industries to set beauty standards to help us visualize the "beautiful people" and long to be like them. Fitness, entertainment, beauty, fashion, and social media help connect us to all attractions deemed *sexy*.

With that said, men still have the need for women. Innately, they realize they need help. Our world teaches this in a negative fashion, which reflects the deceivers' design to make having help as useless as possible. It is perverted; but confused women take pride in landing the catch (the man) and having an affirming experience, even though it may be short-lived and not too meaningful. They may still say, "I am attractive, so I will keep it up."

Another point of deception is the Cinderella story, where a woman or a young girl lacks most things, but her goal is to meet the man who will sweep her off her feet, and they will live happily ever after. She feels she must always reflect that beautiful, appealing image. Unfortunately, this opens her up to everyone and everything. She cannot mind her business and focus on the big picture, because she thinks she must be available. This is like the loose woman referred to in the Book of Proverbs, warning a good man to beware. Some women experience multiple pregnancies and several children, however, that does not stop them from continuing their search and hope for their prince to appear. Sons of men see this effort and take full advantage of the situation.

Unmarried women who do not see themselves as Helpers married to Christ are pawns for Satan to destroy. Destruction is on many levels: men, children, family, organizations, and themselves.

Men who do not see themselves as Adams, sons of the living God, are also pawns of Satan. They are belittled, fearful, and nailed down to earthly activities without godly vision. With little to no real power, they are being crushed by women and fighting the unwinnable fight against Satan's world system without Christ, our soon coming King, and God of the angel armies.

A man in Christ who seeks God for his Helper is off to a good start in life.

Main Points:

- All females are, by nature, God-designed Helpers.
- A man in Christ who seeks God for his Helper is off to a good start in life.

My Testimony: The Story of the Great Bleed

CHAPTER 12

※

My Testimony: The Story of the Great Bleed

In 2017, I fell sick to a brain bleed. I asked God to heal me in Jesus' Name. I realized that my healing process had immediately begun. The Father had begun to answer my prayers. However, my healing was not happening the way I had scripted the outcome. I was thinking that my healing would be like the snap of a finger from the divine hand of God. This would simply reset and restore my left side, making it totally functional, allowing me to get back in the saddle of life. It would allow me to continue moving forward with slight increments of positive progress to bring *great* glory to His Name.

But what I have received, to date, is a divinely crafted healing strategy that could have only been masterminded by the hand of God. Looking at this carefully implemented experience, there was much healing needed in my personality, values, and understanding of what is most important in life. The Healer needed to clarify who was in charge and responsible for preparing me for that great return of our Lord without shame, embarrassment, or fault.

I was an arrogant mess. I had a daily devotion-in-a-box that kept me afloat. I was popular for my accomplishments in the wellness industry, and I was a Bible teacher, consistent worshipper, tither, and I gave to the poor. However, as the healing continued, I discovered pockets of unfruitful acts and thoughts that were not bringing glory to God. I discovered generational curses, disrespectful positions toward my husband and marriage, and a total lack of wisdom, which is needed to live greatly for God. I had the position that my works, not my faith, drove everything and should be acceptable to God. I took "the way that seemed right" and ended up being divinely strapped into a cocoon for learning, correction, and growth.

Everything has changed. To encourage me, God gave me visions, dreams, and a desire to see myself walking and functioning whole, so I knew that healing would be made visible.

My hope and attitude became one of gratitude for the overwhelming showers of grace and love from the Father. I was on a blank canvas. The new beginning started with releasing the old *me* by diving into the Word of God and asking for an understanding of how to apply the Living Word to myself. I cannot explain what applying this healing balm to my diseased spirit has accomplished. God strategically healed or made corrections to my body so I could sit properly with Him. For example, I could eat and see, and I had full memory, intellect, and speech.

The Lord pointed me to several books written by anointed men and women of God. He took me to a set of preachers and teachers of scripture who helped me take in even more wisdom and understanding of His Word to uproot trees and bad vineyards in my heart (soul) and mind.

My faith was making me whole. I had switched from living as a carnal Christian to becoming a Spirit-filled believer in the Lord Jesus

Christ. I now have His love with enough to share. I realized that God loved me from the beginning and gave me enough love to care for me and others.

I have the grace of God, which humbles me and allows me to show grace to others. I understand forgiveness and can now forgive and forget. My new prayer life has given me a relationship with the Trinity of God that surpasses all understanding. I have been freed from my feeble attempts at being a woman of God. Now, I am a daughter of God, full of faith, who is heir to the throne and at peace with the will of God and His Kingdom so I can live and move and have my being. My being was planned, architected, and constructed with what gets me to *me*, in love.

Because of His grace, there are loop routines that kick in every time I decide to go, or get caught off course. These loops of grace provide a way out of the situation, an altar for cleansing, and the path to the way of correction, which is also gentle and loving. It sounds unbelievable. Yes, in my unbelief, I would have agreed. But now that I have fully been in the Love of God, I can say that it is "very believable." John 15:1 presents God the Father as the Gardener. He knows how to make the branches grow that are attached to Jesus, the Christ, as the Vine.

I have realized that this experience has been so special and gentle. It has been an easy yoke and a light burden. From the Intensive Care Unit, enduring two brain surgeries, convalescing stays, and now being kept and sheltered by my incredible Adam (my husband, my gift, and the strong man chosen to cover and nurture me), has been a blessed experience. His love for his God and for me has allowed my healing to go forth unhindered and fruitful.

My prayers became *Yes!* I asked Holy Spirit to help me and prepare me for my full healing. This healing journey for me was a spiritual first. I have been scrubbed up spiritually with a complete overhaul of direction. I have had my purpose aired, shaken, and repositioned.

Now, I am still and practicing being in the presence of God with Christ. I am convinced that His way is the only way for me. His plan is the only plan for me. His will is the only will for me. His desire for my life is the light and life for all I do, and impossible without His strength and joy. His Word and wonder are overwhelming for me. Holy Spirit provides the portion I need for each day.

How could I, as a believer, be so saturated with unbelief, self-righteousness, and disobedience? How could I have mastered maintaining a little light in my soul instead of permitting the explosive well to spring up? How could I not see and embrace all the good that was hovering over me, waiting for the opportunity to move into my brokenness?

My high-strung temperament and doing the "my way" type of living caused the brain bleed. One day after not getting my way, my blood pressure went high enough to cause a thinning of blood vessels and the wall of one vessel in my brain gave way, and a hole was created causing a bleed. I was annoyed, closing the kitchen after dinner, and then it happened.

The next event was, at the time, the loving promise I needed. I see now that it has changed and matured my thinking in an amazing way. In the ambulance, on the way to the hospital, I was in and out of consciousness. I heard the voice of my Lord say, "Just relax, I've got this." I drifted off into a state of rest. Looking back on the situation, I know the Father saw what was happening. He did not ignore the opportunity to use this situation for my good and His glory. His Word says that what the enemy does for bad, God will use it for good. (Genesis 50:20). So be clear, God did not cause my brain bleed. He took advantage of a bad situation and made it good.

My Adam was standing at his post, loving me as Christ loves the Church, making a special tent for me within his household like Isaac did for Rebekah (Genesis 24:67), and I began to heal. It was like a special invitation from the Father to sit with the Spirit of God to learn His way and purpose for my life.

Finally, II Peter 3:8 states, "But, beloved, be not ignorant of this one thing, that one day is with the Lord as a thousand years, and a thousand years as one day." I can say that I have been sitting for a little over five years (or 1,825 days), and if I could complete my assignment just sitting with Him, I would continue to do it. But I have an Adam and I must lean into this assignment for him so that he can complete his work.

So why am I taking you through this story? This is *my* story; you will not need to go through anything close to this to get to your office. This testimony will encourage you to sit with our Lord *before* hitting a wall.

Lessons Learned (or reinforced)

Eve (me)

1. The full biblical connection to my Adam. I honor him.
2. Adam leads me as God leads him.
3. I am not in control. I help.
4. My supernatural connection to God's Holy Spirit sustains me.
5. I am constantly connected to Holy Spirit help for my Adam.
6. I override human instinct and do good.

My Adam

1. The full biblical connection to my Eve.
2. I am a son of God and follow my elder brother, Jesus.
3. I love Eve the way Christ loves the Church; He died for her.
4. I am a prince robed in Righteousness, carrying Love and Peace.
5. I cover my household.
6. Eve has a leadership role in our household, with God, for us.

FREQUENTLY ASKED QUESTIONS ABOUT THE OFFICE OF EVE

FAQ 01 — What is the daily activity of Eve?

FAQ 02 — What if I have no desire for an Adam?

FAQ 03 — What if I desire an Adam, but don't have one?

FAQ 04 — How should I pray for my Adam?

FAQ 05 — What is the cookie jar? How can I have one? (Finances)

FAQ 06 — How does this apply to blended families (covenant marriages)?

FAQ 07 — What if I need help with my Adam?

FAQ 08 — What if my Adam is not following Christ?

FAQ 09 — How do I handle church hurt?

FAQ 10 — What about my Adam relative to other Helpers?

FAQ 11 — What if I am divorced?

FREQUENTLY ASKED QUESTIONS ABOUT THE OFFICE OF EVE

FAQ 01 — What is the daily activity of Eve?

Eve rises early to embrace "this is the day" that the Lord has made. She receives the perfection of the gift of "this day." Her joy overflows into the household. She speaks life and not death. This day.

She prays targeted prayers for her Adam, starting with the prayer of Jabez in I Chronicles 4:9-10, to cover his household and dominion. She completes her to-do list and then submits it to the Lord. Her fellowship with Holy Spirit gives the guidance, instruction, and wisdom from the least to the largest challenges of the day. As she leans on Him, those difficult things become possible.

She is prayed up and ready to minister to Adam and make sure every need is met. She listens and enjoys their time together. She gets to collect prayer points for Adam with every encounter. His frustrations and challenges are her concern. Little goes unnoticed with this sister.

Her prayer life restores enough love for every assignment.

She has prayer with close sisters in Christ and agrees with them in prayer for various things, from children, household, and meals to community projects as led by Holy Spirit.

FAQ 02 — What if I have no desire for an Adam?

If you have no desire to be married, then you are one of the blessed singles who can proceed under the sole banner of Jesus Christ. The Apostle Paul and Jesus shares words about this, which is basically, "single is great" in God! (I Corinthians 7:7-9)

A single Helper who agrees to grow (prosper) her soul, takes on the "this mind" of Christ and gives full reign of her life to God, Holy Spirit, is one of the most powerful humans remaining in the universe.

FAQ 03 — What if I desire an Adam, but don't have one?

You always have an Adam. Every born-again Helper is spiritually married to Christ, as stated in scripture. I know this current age encourages us to desire a human male, Adam.

Know that the deceiver can create a desire to be married based on a strong physical, sexual expression of passion and emotion, which is not a Helper assignment. If not checked, and Satan gets your attention, these feelings can fester and lead your heart away from God, putting you right at sin's door. It can become all-consuming. Every thought can lead to *a longing* to be married. But you can *see* the lie and avoid much drama.

If God planted this desire within your heart, you could make your list for an Adam and pray over it, giving it to God. (*See* FAQ 04 — How should I pray for my Adam?) If you believe God heard your prayer, then you can go to rest with this. This rest removes the anxiousness, thoughts, and triggers that take you out of faith. You don't have to worry because your Father has this now. Now, you can restore your position in God by reading Psalm 139 and Jeremiah 29:11. Your purpose is, "I help in the context of God's plan for my life." Your life is like an interview.

You are *24/7,* demonstrating to God your understanding of Him in your life and His best work within every stage of your life.

Avoid the triggers, which are those thoughts and situations that bring on those "poor lonely me" feelings from people, places, or things, like movies and romantic events. These feelings can also make you vulnerable to more evil situations than you would normally avoid.

Know that Christ takes those thoughts and that energy and transforms them into what pleases Him. Christ's agenda is far bigger than that. Your commitment to Christ provides a mark of distinction, which over time makes you a prize and available to have a life in the physical with an Adam, son of God. Also, know that Christ loves you so much that what He wants for you will also please you.

FAQ 04 – How should I pray for my Adam?

You must **see** the answer to your prayer **before** you receive the answer. We do not live by chance, but by the Word and will of God.

In David Cho's book, *The Fourth Dimension,* he points out the importance of praying specifically for your Adam. You have preferences, so include them with the petition for your Adam. Write down the answers to these questions to help. For example:

- What race or ethnic background?
- Tall, as in six feet or short, as in five feet?
- Slim and trim or pleasantly plump?
- What kind of hobby should he have?
- What kind of job or vocation?
- What about His walk with God?

Tape this list on your mirror and thankfully read it every day.

Read these answers aloud and use your prayerful imagination to see him! You could add more items, if desired. Now that you see him, you know what to ask God for. God does not provide what you cannot see. So, Father, in Jesus' Name, we order this Adam. Thank you.

Now remember, you are a Helper. But you do *not* have to help the Father answer this prayer. When He needs your help, He will let you know.

God will prepare you and him for this answered prayer.

<u>Other possible details to consider for your order</u>:

- Loves the Lord Jesus
- Loves the Word (The Bible or God's Voice)
- Mannerisms – those you like
- Good steward of finances
- Very knowledgeable
- Well read
- Well spoken
- Knows that he is a king/leader
- Will love you as Christ loves the Church
- Loves children
- Can cook
- Cares

Thank you, Holy Spirit, for giving me the desires that allowed me to make these petitions by faith, in Jesus' Name. Amen.

Assessing Adam for marriage:

1. What is it that you are being asked to attach yourself to?
2. Can Jesus be connected also?

3. What is the work for a Helper that is connected to this guy?
   a. Note: The work relates to his purpose in life or his calling.
   b. The work is not getting him saved or changing a fixer upper.
4. Is he a kingdom leader? Or is he primarily seeking to cover his sex drive so as not to *burn*, according to scripture?

FAQ 05 – What is the cookie jar? How can I have one? (Finances)

Make sure that the household is tithing. If not, there are blockages to your obedience, go to Holy Spirit and Adam for leadership (in that order), in Jesus' Name. This one act of obedience brings in every promise associated with the blessing of the Lord. You allow God to intensify His good all over your life. (Malachi 3:8).

Your cookie jar is the treasury for the household that is expected of a wise woman who builds her house, according to Proverbs 14:1. It is a set-aside fund that starts small and builds as your territory grows. It does not take away from the household funds but can be used to support house efforts and spur-of-the-moment uses. It should be used as a seed toward projects as assigned. Your portfolio of assignments will increase the treasury. Do not see this as a petty cash fund. Why? Because large works will come through this powerful but simple jar.

This fund is not Eve's income. It is solely for fruitful activities and will multiply for all such projects by faith.

FAQ 06 – How does this apply to blended
families (covenant marriages)?

Many marriages have difficult beginnings because the oneness brings all the parts together spiritually. They must be seen that way.

The glue of the family is far from being a biological connection. If the leader and his Helper are in Christ, the oneness is made possible.

Blended families must embrace this quickly. This is because of the uprooting of dead trees in the hearts and minds of all involved that needs to take place. It will take some time to shape this precious new family. The Word of God is what supernaturally uses love *not* to blend together broken pieces, but to make all pieces whole and then blend them together into perfection.

Your unique prayer points:

- Pray for your Adam's leadership and your followership.
- In prayer, ask for customized love for each family member.
- Open your eyes of understanding about each family member.
- Establish a family prayer circle.
- Pray for salvation where it is missing.
- Exercise faith for every relationship, interaction, and experience, using the uniqueness of love for each relationship.
- Pray for the supernatural development of your Adam's household.
- Pray for protection against fiery darts.

Other things to consider on your watch:

- Stay in love. No anger. Take all wounds and offenses to God. See the enemy. Love must be gentle but tough. Love is not a doormat.
- Discuss challenges with your Adam.
- Implement family prayer time, reading scripture, and personal prayer.
- Be available to suggest a Christian counselor.
- Respond to other promptings and leadings of Holy Spirit.

- Stay above the pettiness.
- Remember that pain inflicts pain.

"Calm comes as healing happens." —*Surina Jordan*

FAQ 07 – What if I need help with my Adam?

I am married to a godly man. However, to me, he is sometimes a loving *knuckle head*. We see things differently.

You and he have different perspectives on most things. It is important, however, that you do not pull away. Instead, pull together in the same direction, although in different ways. In other words, have discussions knowing that you need to end up in a certain place — whatever that place is — although you're probably going to get there differently. Holy Spirit understands this situation also. You are kind of backing into where you both need to be, but as you circle around with the spirit of good communication, you can see how you both land where you need to, and continue to be one.

When Adam does not embrace his position and love you biblically, I highly suggest that you go to God the Helper concerning him, as soon as possible.

Resist fussing to your kids about their father or chatting with a girlfriend about the shortcomings of your husband. This approach is not recommended because your words may slip and open a door to the enemy.

Know that God made men, who are by nature, to be acknowledged and honored, but not without help.

As you pray, you are praying for yourself because in the spirit realm, God sees you two as one. If your husband is not in Christ, your first petition is for his salvation.

Because your awesomeness would disrupt the earth, Adam is given dominion before you.

FAQ 08 — What if my Adam is not following Christ?

Scripture clearly says that your life and walk with God can sanctify your husband and you can grow peaceably. (I Corinthians 7:14).

However, if you are in an abusive situation, you are free to separate as you are led. Know that your Heavenly Father will not have you trapped in a hellish environment. If you are being mentally or physically abused by your Adam, do not be confused about what you should do. You are a Helper, but the *sickness* in Adam does not recognize who you are, why he needs you, or why he must value you highly.

If you end up maimed, disabled, or dead, what is your assignment? Or, if you are beginning to think this mistreatment is your fault, how can you help?

In the *Love* commandment, it states we are to love others as we love ourselves. If your Adam is not able to love you, it indicates that self-hate is within him. Please go to Holy Spirit ask for clarity and the path to resolve this. Now!

Pray as a daughter of the King. Use His Words, and by faith, speak the good that must happen. In other words, pray the solution, *not* the problem. Holy Spirit can fix this, but you cannot.

Meanwhile, continue to do your praise and worship and meditate on appropriate scripture. Jesus will show you the way out or through. Pray for God's hedge of protection around you and your children. Pray that God will keep you from evil.

FAQ 09 — How do I handle church hurt?

Who wins from you walking away from your spiritual home? How many laws of God have been thrown to the garbage because of this? Whatever *this* is, you will need to put a value on it and decide if it is worth it.

For example, the Word of God says, "Not forsaking the assembling of ourselves together, as the manner of some is; but exhorting one another: and so much the more, as ye see the day approaching." (Hebrews 10:25).— **Continue to gather with other children of God.**

Next, the Word of God points to the love triangle that underscores the relationships essential to how love is worked through the Christ's Body. (Matthew 22:37-40). He said, "By this shall all men know that ye are my disciples, if ye have love one to another." (John 13:35). — **Continue to be loving.**

The Word of God tells us to forgive those who trespass against us. (Matthew 6:14). — **Continue to forgive.**

And lastly, we are told in the Word of God to tithe. (Malachi 3:8-10). Being in a church setting contains all the acts of obedience that can be accomplished. Giving is not to a personality, but unto God. — **Continue to give.**

Who wins from you walking away from your spiritual home? **The enemy does.**

Fiery darts of the wicked come. This attack typically comes when you least expect it and from a direction that is least expected. It hurts for these reasons, but also if it comes in the area where your soul and your spirit are exposed (church), because only good is supposed to be there.

As a result, a hurt of this nature can do almost permanent damage and cause one to leave the church and have their light go dim as they forsake the assembly with the fellowship. These hurts can come from the leadership or a group of helpful Helpers or a ministry. It can result in not being accepted, not being supported, children being mistreated, or lack of training and teaching.

So, as you heal and forgive, you can open yourself up to the love and healing nature of God. He may lead you to another fellowship that is stronger and whole. Or He could send you right back to the fellowship you walked away from. Your obedience to "not forsake" gathering is clearing the way for proper order in your life. Pray about every step you take.

FAQ 10 — What about my Adam relative to other Helpers?

Adam is to always be respected; however, no one should honor him the way *you* do.

Eve should not expect another Helper to see her Adam like she does. He is off limits. It is important that you understand you are *not* to see and honor another Adam as you see and honor *your* Adam. Other Adams are seen as your brothers in Christ. A brother Adam is not your leader. You have only one Adam. *He* is your assignment.

FAQ 11 – What if I am divorced?

Good question. When you accept Christ, all things become new. Whatever your past, God's Word says that in Christ we are *new* creatures. (II Corinthians 5:17). So, you have Christ as your Lord, Savior, and now husband. This is a good place to be.

Prayer Toolkit

Extra Help for Helpers — (A) Connect to Christ

Extra Help for Helpers — (B) Prayer Scripts

01 - Prayer to Accept the Office of Eve

02 - Prayer for Eve, Married to Christ

03 - Prayer for Eve, Married to Adam

04 - Prayer to Overcome Weaknesses

05 - Prayer to Overcome Mistakes

06 - Prayer to Overcome Fear

07 - Prayer for Adam

08 - Prayer for Your Adam (Christ)

09 - Prayer to Receive My Adam (Husband)

10 - Prayer of Preparation to Receive My Adam

11 - Prayer of Preparation for Comfort with Adam

12 - A Mother's Prayer for her Son (Adam)

13 - A Mother's Prayer for her Daughter (Helper)

14 - Prayer for My Heart's Desire

15 - Prayer for Proper Alignment of Marriage

16 - Prayer for a Commitment to the Office

17 - Prayer for The Wisdom of God

18 - Prayer for Troubled Marriages

19 - Prayer of Thanksgiving for Godly Marriages

20 - Prayer for a Marriage that Needs Changes

21 - Prayer for "Out of Church Fellowship"

22 - Prayer for The Church

Extra Help for Helpers — (C) Proverbs 31 Woman

Extra Help for Helpers — (D) My Vow

- Married to Adam
- Married to Jesus

Extra Help For Helpers
(A) Connect to Christ

Prayer to Accept Christ.

Instruction: Read this out loud.

Dear Jesus, I come to You now, asking You to forgive me for my sins. I believe the Gospel of Jesus Christ, that He suffered, bled, and died for me. I believe Jesus rose and brought full restoration for all who believe. Come into my heart and live in me through Your Holy Spirit. Help me to learn and grow in this new life. Teach me how to become the Helper You have in mind for me. Thank You for being the perfect God who wants a relationship with the imperfect me.

Romans 10:9 states, "that if thou shalt *confess* with thy mouth the Lord Jesus, and shalt *believe* in thine heart that God hath raised him from the dead, thou shalt *be saved.*"

I confess; I believe; and I receive this gift of salvation. Thank You, in Jesus' Name. Amen.

Congratulations! You just did the most wonderful
thing in your life, *for* your life!

Go back to the section entitled,
"Now that you have Christ in your life"
to continue your new journey.

Extra Help For Helpers (B) Prayer Scripts

01 — Prayer to Accept the Office of Eve

Lord God, I never realized how scripture includes women in such a powerful way. If I will embrace Your will and put my faith in You to see the power You gave to me in Genesis 1:28, and again in Acts 2:1-4, I will unlock my future and my ability to bring You more complete glory. This path through everlasting life is believably awesome. You are God and You thought about me before You designed me. According to Jeremiah 1:5, You have a history of designing us. In Psalm 139, You watched over Your design (me) as I grew in the womb, and You gave me purpose.

Father, thank You. I am Eve restored by Christ. My office is connected to Proverbs 31. Now I have The Way to go, The Truth to keep life plain, and I have The Life. I accept the plan and purpose You have for me. In Jesus' Name. Amen.

02 — Prayer for Eve, Married to Christ

For thy Maker is thine husband; the LORD of hosts is his name;
and thy Redeemer the Holy One of Israel;
The God of the whole earth shall he be called. —Isaiah 54:5

Dear Father God, this is Eve, here for my Adam, Christ Jesus, Your firstborn. Thank You for this awesome assignment to be connected to my Adam, Jesus. Help me learn about those things closest to His heart and those things that are His work, like the Church and various ministries. Prepare me, Holy Spirit, to receive my assignments. In Jesus' Name. Amen.

03 — Prayer for Eve, Married to Adam

Father, in Jesus' Name, thank You for teaching me that I need to walk into the Office of Eve. An army of Eves in the world is what we need to glorify You. Be it unto me. Genesis 1:27 says I was made in the image of the Holy Trinity: God the Father, God the Son, and God, Holy Spirit. Thank You for creating me, a Helper. You have blessed me and empowered me to lead, to be fruitful [productive], to multiply and to have dominion over the earth. I ask You for wisdom, understanding, and revelation of Your Word. Help me to walk in The Way, the Truth, and The Life. Thank you for letting me be quick to hear, slow to speak, slow to become angry. (James 1:19). I confess that I will do good and not evil to Adam all the days of my life. (Proverbs 31:12). In Jesus' Name. Amen.

04 — Prayer to Overcome Weaknesses

Thanks for getting me here and for releasing me from this world's approach to life for women and girls. Thank You that Your Word assures me, Your grace is sufficient for me, for Christ's strength is made perfect in weakness. (II Corinthians 12:9). It is so good to know that in my weakness, be it mind, body, or spirit, You become strong, according to this Word. I trust in You, and I am helped. Thank You for an ordered "what next." In Jesus' Name. Amen.

05 — Prayer to Overcome Mistakes

In the Office of Eve, in concept, it is clear to me that I need to remain in my office totally relying on God, Holy Spirit, the Helper, for help. Thank you for this assignment. I confess that it seems so overwhelming, near impossible, and I am making mistakes. But Your Word says in Luke 1:37, "For with God nothing shall be impossible." I receive and believe this Word. In Jesus' Name. Amen.

06 — Prayer to Overcome Fear

God, Thank you for Your Word that says You have not given us the spirit of fear but of power and love and of a sound mind. (II Timothy 1:7). And you continue to admonish us to "not be afraid." Thank You, that the mind of Christ in me, by faith, makes me above this world. Help us to resist the devil, so he will flee from us. No sickness, disease, hurt, harm, or danger has any power over us (Adam and me) or our household. In Jesus' Name. Amen.

07 — Prayer for Adam

Dear Father, thank You for this revelation of how You operate. Thank You for my Adam. I do not understand it all, but You are loving and patient throughout my life if I yield. Thanks for assuring me that I do not have to be perfect, but rather, aligned with Christ for salvation and righteousness. Thank You. In Jesus' Name. Amen.

08 — Prayer for your Adam (Christ)

I offer praise because Jesus is Lord and His Blood restored me to the Office of Eve in Christ. Give me respect and honor for my Christ and His love for You, Father. As Christ prayed; "Thy Kingdom come, thy will be done, on earth as it is in heaven." (Matthew 6:10). Holy Spirit, Christ's body (the Church) all pastors, ministers, and ministries, local and global, need your help. Please anoint, restore, and renew us in the spirit of our minds. We pray for the suffering, leaders in the church, the less fortunate, workers for Christ, and the causes of Christ. Thank You. I love You, Eve. In Jesus' Name. Amen.

09 — Prayer to Receive My Adam (Husband)

Father God, I have so many images of meeting a guy and getting married. Marriage is somewhat unsettling. In Jesus' Name, I ask You to prepare me for the assignment of marriage. In this world, it appears I've got myself all together. However, I am out of shape spiritually. I yield to You for a total spiritual, mental, and emotional makeover. In Jesus' Name. Amen.

10 — Prayer of Preparation to Receive My Adam

Father, I pray that You would not only prepare me, but please prepare Adam for me. I pray that his life experiences are exactly what are needed for him to be my husband — a man who is strong in the Lord, loves and respects his Savior and brother Jesus, and who is operating in his office as king, in need of me, his Helper. In Jesus' Name. Amen.

11 — Prayer of Preparation for Comfort with Adam

Father, I need a man who I am so comfortable with that I can be here with You and almost not know he is here — we can be together without being away from You. We are most comfortable in fellowship with God, Holy Spirit. Your Word says, "For this reason a man will leave his father and mother and be united to his wife, and the two will become one flesh. So they are no longer two, but one flesh." (Mark 10:7-8). I receive that comfort through Your Word. In Jesus' Name. Amen.

12 — A Mother's Prayer for her Son (Adam)

Father, this is Eve on behalf of my son, who is Adam. Thank You for all the good that is in place to help him. Until he is assigned an Eve, I pray for Holy Spirit's leadership and assistance every day of his life. Thank You for preparing a Helper for him.

The enemy of God has studied my son to destroy him, but we pray Your hedge of protection around him, in Jesus' Name. I will not be afraid, and You will help us. (Isaiah 41:13). Bring him good friends, as You did for David and Jonathan in scripture. Father, you wrote the book in heaven about my son, Adam. I ask that You lead me as his Helper until you assign a Helper to him. Help me to stay silent and be observant. Help me be prepared to see the traps and weapons being used by the enemy to destroy him. Thank You. In Jesus' Name. Amen.

13 — A Mother's Prayer for her Daughter (Helper)

Dear Father, in Jesus' Name, this is Eve coming to you on behalf of the daughter (Helper) whom you have entrusted to me. She has always been a precious gift in Your sight and You and I both love her. Holy Spirit, I pray for my daughter, a Helper. I ask that You help us guard her imagination and seal all open portals and exposures to her mind and spirit that she may remain holy and upright in her ways. I acknowledge the divine office that you ordained from the beginning. I pray that she becomes your bride until you assign her to her Adam. Thank You. In Jesus' Name. Amen.

14 — Prayer for My Heart's Desire

"Father, I thank You that Your Word says, "take delight in the Lord, and he will give you the *desires of your heart.*" (Psalm 37:4). Remove every desire in my heart that You did not plant. Grant me now, these desires. I receive them now by faith, with joy, for You are my delight. Your Word does not change. I believe, I receive. In Jesus' Name. Amen.

15 — Prayer for Proper Alignment of Marriage

Lord, open my spiritual eyes that I might see and my spiritual ears that I might hear Your way. I ask for wisdom to do life with full understanding as a Proverbs 31 wife. Holy Spirit, I need Your help. Prepare my Adam for Your change in us. Thank You. In Jesus' Name. Amen.

16 — Prayer for a Commitment to the Office

In the Kingdom of God, life gets more doable and simpler as we learn more of the Word of God and His promises. All the fear and confusion go away. The low self-esteem and not being good enough… gone.

Thank You for this revelation of the Office of Eve. It is so *You*. It is so wonderful to see Your thoughts and the ambitions You have in mind for me, a woman You have kept and looked after for all these years. There is a release that happens within Your spirit that validates my existence, by faith. We move with it from faith to faith, according to Romans 1:17, as we continue to grow. I commit to go into my office with the Holy Spirit of God's Help.

Thank You for not looking at my sins and shortcomings. Now, I know that with Jesus and Your Word, there is nothing impossible for me to do! NO-thing! Love you lots. In Jesus' Name. Amen.

17 – Prayer for the Wisdom of God

Father, in Jesus' Name, Your Word in James 1:5 says, "If any of you lack wisdom, let him ask of God, that giveth to all men liberally …and shall be given him." I ask You for wisdom now, according to Your Word, which says "Get wisdom, get understanding…" (Proverbs 4:5). I also ask that You allow me to get understanding along with the wisdom. Thank you. In Jesus' Name. Amen.

18 — Prayer for Troubled Marriages

Dear Father, I need Your help. In our marriage, we are not *one*, according to Mark 10:8. We do not get the full picture of marriage Your way. Now we are midstream, and You are not being glorified. Help me, help us to correct things and experience the love, peace and joy that has been here for us all along. No more deception. No more selfishness and no fear. No more "*my* way."

Holy Spirit, this is Eve, for my Adam. I pray that You would help him be the leader. I pray that You would open our eyes to see him as the leader. We pray for wisdom and understanding. We pray for eyes that see and ears that hear. We pray for a prayer life together and Bible study habits. Help us not to compare or compete and to only remember the good.

Help us to love You more and in Your love, let us see how to love each other. I receive this good and perfect gift of marriage from You. Help us to allow You to perfect it. Thank You. In Jesus' Name. Amen.

19 — Prayer of Thanksgiving for Godly Marriages

Father, since we are both in Christ, we pray for a sustainable relationship. We thank You for the beautiful years of marriage. Glory to Your Name. In Jesus' Name. Amen.

20 — Prayer for a Marriage that Needs Changes

Father, Thank You for this Word. It is just in time to save my marriage. I never considered having a prayer life just for my Adam. However, if I am the Helper assigned to him, connected to Holy Spirit, we need a oneness mindset. If he can love me as Christ loves the Church, unconditionally, then I can honor him with an "as-is" approach under You, Dear Father. I can pray for his leadership and our ability to see each other as treasures, gifts from You. Thank you for helping us see and hear with our spiritual eyes and ears.

In Jesus' Name, we come against all evil and any weapons formed against us. We come against anger, unforgiveness, self-righteousness, and pride. We come against any other relationship that is blocking our desire for oneness. Your Word in Psalm 138:8 says, "The Lord will perfect that which concerneth me: thy mercy, O Lord, endureth for ever: forsake not the works of thine own hands." I ask for more wisdom, understanding, and help seeing The Way for me to get on the path carved out for me and my assignment. Thank You that Adam loves me like he loves himself, according to Ephesians 5:33. Thank You. In Jesus' Name. Amen.

21 — Prayer for "Out of Church Fellowship"

Father, we are no longer members of a church fellowship. For whatever the reason, it is beginning to look more like the hand of the deceiver. Your Word says in Hebrews 10:25 that we should not forsake the assembling of ourselves together. Help me not be so critical or use an unholy imagination against Your people. This one act of obedience to You is a good first step to heal all the brokenness in our marriage that we cannot see. Thank You for making room for our gifts within this fellowship and for affirming my Adam as the leader of his household and me as his Helper. In Jesus' Name. Amen.

22 — Prayer for The Church

Father, we pray for every Eve within the Body of Christ, called the Church. We pray for the proper alignment of Helpers and Adams in the Church. We pray for Your kingdom to come, and Your will to be done on earth as it is in heaven. We pray for a supernatural intervention into the Church. We pray for church leadership, every ministry and pew member. We pray new life for every Helper. Holy Spirit, not our will, but Your will be done in the Church of Jesus Christ. In Jesus' Name. Amen.

Extra Help For Helpers
(C) The Proverbs 31 Woman

Verses 10-31

---

10 Who can find a virtuous woman? for her price is far above rubies.

11 The heart of her husband doth safely trust in her, so that he shall have no need of spoil.

12 She will do him good and not evil all the days of her life.

13 She seeketh wool, and flax, and worketh willingly with her hands.

14 She is like the merchants' ships; she bringeth her food from afar.

15 She riseth also while it is yet night, and giveth meat to her household, and a portion to her maidens.

16 She considereth a field, and buyeth it: with the fruit of her hands she planteth a vineyard.

17 She girdeth her loins with strength, and strengtheneth her arms.

18 She perceiveth that her merchandise is good: her candle goeth not out by night.

19 She layeth her hands to the spindle, and her hands hold the distaff.

20 She stretcheth out her hand to the poor; yea, she reacheth forth her hands to the needy.

21 She is not afraid of the snow for her household: for all her household are clothed with scarlet.

22 She maketh herself coverings of tapestry; her clothing is silk and purple.

23 Her husband is known in the gates, when he sitteth among the elders of the land.

24 She maketh fine linen, and selleth it; and delivereth girdles unto the merchant.

25 Strength and honour are her clothing; and she shall rejoice in time to come.

26 She openeth her mouth with wisdom; and in her tongue is the law of kindness.

27 She looketh well to the ways of her household, and eateth not the bread of idleness.

28 Her children arise up, and call her blessed; her husband also, and he praiseth her.

29 Many daughters have done virtuously, but thou excellest them all.

30 Favour is deceitful, and beauty is vain: but a woman that feareth the Lord, she shall be praised.

31 Give her of the fruit of her hands; and let her own works praise her in the gates.

Extra Help for Helpers
(D) My Vows

Let the Lord lead you and construct the vow for *your* life. This is my vow, feel free to modify it to create yours.

My Vow to God – Married to Adam

Father, in Jesus' Name, because You have made me whole, with the complete manifested healing (body, mind, and spirit), I make the following vow to you:

1. All my endeavors must flow out of Adam's territory. (Proverbs 31).
2. Go tell whomever, wherever, whenever in the order of Melchizedek, on my way, which is Your way for me. (Matthew 28:19).
3. I will pursue a prospering soul through the Word of God and remain in the Office of Eve, according to III John 1:2.
4. I will honor my Adam by Your spirit as Sarah's daughter according to I Peter 3:6.
5. I will do him good all the days of my life, according to Proverbs 31:10-12.

Love, in Jesus' Name. Amen.

My Vow to God – Married to Jesus

Father God, I come in Jesus' Name, the One who has restored my relationship with You and who has pledged before You to be my husband. I now make the following vow to Jesus to be my Lord, Savior, and husband. Because You have made me whole, and have made me free from all unholiness, I present myself to His Majesty with a good and perfect heart. With Your strength, and Holy Spirit help, I make the following vow to You:

1. All my endeavors must flow out of Jesus' territory. (Proverbs 31).
2. Go tell whomever, wherever, whenever in the order of Melchizedek, on my way, which is Your way for me. (Matthew 28:19).
3. I will pursue a prospering soul through the Word of God and will remain strong and wise within the Office of Eve, according to III John 1:2.
4. I will honor my Jesus by Your Spirit, as Sarah's daughter, according to I Peter 3:6.
5. I will do Jesus good all the days of my life, according to Proverbs 31:12.

Love, in Jesus' Name. Amen.

Afterword

You cannot replace your value to God, His desire, and vision for your life.

We must be **INTENTIONAL** about embracing our placement here on earth. Look at the time and relevancy of the day in which you have been placed. As we number our days, your value and your desires will become clear as you grow in God (as your soul prospers).

I spent years trying to be what other people were. I even decided to select what I considered the good things about each person and include them in my mixed bag of a plan. Included in this bag was my obsession with self-help *everything*. A very good earthly strategy but barely salvageable from a Kingdom of God perspective.

This conversation appears strangely like a weave of going in and out of the natural realm into the spirit realm. But the reality is that things most important in your life have direct spiritual origins. Your faith in Christ and His gospel is what strengthens your ability to reach for the next. Your faith will allow you to embrace the Book of Genesis, Chapter 1 (the creation story) and see your value. The Office of Eve begins to appear.

It also becomes clear that we are **spirit first**, made in the image of God, wrapped in flesh, and given the breath of life. The Word of God tells us to come to Him in **spirit** and truth. The Spirit of Wisdom and Truth will always help the Helpers in Christ.

Caring for Christ and His world (sphere) is a great assignment to have. As we seek Holy Spirit for help in helping our Adam, God's Word, which is the presence of Christ, will prosper our souls and yield good health. (III John 1:2).

This one understanding of who *you* are as Eve assigned to Adam/Christ liberates you to the Kingdom of God, where plans for you are already completed. Stay on track by literally saying to the deceiver, "I resist you devil, in Jesus' Name." With that said, the devil must get away quickly, erasing all evidence of his trespass with you. (James 4:7).

In your office, live like you have the God of All living life with you.

Surina Ann Jordan, OOE Cofounder

Bibliography

Capps, Charles, ***God's Creative Power for Healing***, Capps Publishing, Broken Arrow, OK, 1991.

Cho, David, ***The Fourth Dimension***, Bridge-Logos Publishers, Newberry, FL, 2020.

About the Author

Surina Ann Jordan is a Christian author who uses her talent and knowledge of the Bible to project biblical messages with profound revelation and truth. She seeks to point to change and its path for proper alignment to Christ. She provides life-changing thoughts that take her audience to their individual crossroads of spiritual protest and elevation.

Unaware of her office for most of her marriage, she has at last lit her Adam's household with more of the Love of God. Her personal motto for a good life is, "Plant the legacy of faith and live the eulogy."

Surina Ann Jordan is pouring out of the well within her heart. She has captured the intended lessons and experiences of her time on earth. She goes deep into the essence of her existence and leans into God to discover purpose and work.

Jordan is a preacher's daughter. She has been a student of the Bible all her life, teaching bible study for many years. She is the founder of the blog, Believers Today.

She earned her PhD in Holistic Nutrition and has over twenty years of experience as a consultant, life coach, vegan chef, public health advocate, and orator. She has written three other books: *The Seven Disciplines of Wellness: The Spiritual Connection to Good Health*, *Living Well: A Series of Short Articles for Holistic Living*, and *Got Cancer? Congratulations! Now You Can Start Living*.

Sheltered by a powerful Adam, Surina Ann Jordan is willing and able to be Eve. Active in the church, she lives out her life focused and committed to her God-given family.

Timeless Treasures

Books by Surina Ann Jordan, OOE, PhD, CLC

Got Cancer? Congratulations!
Now You Can Start Living

The Seven Disciplines of Wellness,
The Spiritual Connection to Good Health

Living Well: A Series of Short Articles for Holistic Living